Praise for Luis Rojas and *The Answer Is Love*

"This is an amazing story of a person who grew up in a middle class family and sought to make his mark in the world. He succeeded in doing so; however, along the way, his success seduced him into a life of darkness. He needed to find self-worth, self-love, and self-esteem to walk out of the dark night of the soul. This book reflects the triumph of his journey of self-discovery, enabling him to stumble and eventually walk back into the light to understand unconditional love. This journey now comes alive so each reader will know there is a life at the end of the tunnel. Luis has now found a way to rebuild his life by dedicating it to helping others walk out of the dark night of the soul. As he points out 'The Answer Is Love.'"

— Dr. Michael Gross, Author of *The Spiritual Primer: Reconnecting to God to Experience Your True Source's Love, Joy, and Happiness*

"*The Answer Is Love* by Luis Rojas is a brave and heartfelt journey toward self-awareness and the realization that in life all we truly need is love. Could not put this amazing book down."

— Linda Gurganus, Nevada

"Luis Rojas is a self-described 'hummingbird' because he will fly above and around a situation, analyzing it from every side until he finds the love in it. The stories in *The Answer Is Love* reflect the wisdom he has gained from this hummingbird behavior, from his days as a prosecuting attorney to personal events filled with abuse, regret, and joy. Readers are in for a rare, insightful treat that will leave them rethinking many of their own attitudes, opinions, and beliefs. Be prepared to experience the evolution of your soul when you read this book."

— Tyler R. Tichelaar, PhD and Award-Winning Author of *Narrow Lives* and *When Teddy Came to Town*

"In *The Answer Is Love,* Luis Rojas shares his inspiring stories and Universe-gifted wisdom to show us that no matter what situation we are in, no matter how difficult or even heinous an experience may be, we always have the opportunity to choose love, and when we do so, healing, hope, and endless possibilities open up for us. This beautiful book will inspire you to choose love daily."

— Susan Friedmann, CPS, International Bestselling Author of Riches in *Niches: How to Make It BIG in a small Market*

"*The Answer Is Love* shows us that love can be at the heart of our destiny if we so choose. Luis Rojas reveals how we can find love in everyday circumstances from going through the drive-thru to soothing our child. His revelations about how to make love the center of our lives are both stunning and bring, deep abiding satisfaction. After reading this book, you will frequently pause throughout your day to take time to find the love in situations, and you will be astounded by the results."

— Patrick Snow, Publishing Coach and International Best-Selling Author of *Creating Your Own Destiny* and *The Affluent Entrepreneur*

THE ANSWER IS Love

A Simple Conversation About Discovering Your True Self

LUIS ROJAS

AVIVA PUBLISHING
New York

THE ANSWER IS LOVE
A Simple Conversation about Discovering Your True Self

Published by:
Aviva Publishing
Lake Placid, NY
(518) 523-1320
www.AvivaPubs.com

Luis Rojas
497 Via Palermo Drive
Henderson, Nevada 89011
702-205-5385
AnswerIsLove.com

ISBN: 978-1-63618-111-0
Library of Congress Control Number: 2021912266

Editors: Tyler Tichelaar and Larry Alexander, Superior Book Productions
Cover and Interior Design: Fusion Creative Works

Every attempt has been made to properly source all quotes.

Although events in this book are based on actual experiences, they reflect the author's memory of the events. Other participants' memories may vary. Names of individuals have been changed to protect their identity and privacy. I have done this because I *Love* and appreciate all of them.

Printed in The United States of America

First Edition

2 4 6 8 10 12

Dedication

To the loves of my life, my two daughters,
May love always be the answer for you.

To you my reader, may this book open your heart to Love.

To my teacher, guru, and dearest friend. Thank you for showing me how to be a man. I will never forget you Danny and the lessons you taught me. May Love always be your guide.

Love, Ray.

To my father, guide,
and dearest friend.
Thank you for showing
me how to be a man.
I will never forget you
During and the lessons
You taught me. May Yours
always be your guide
Jr. 1979.

Acknowledgments

I would like to thank the following people for their contribution to my story, my book, and my life:

To God, thank you for always helping me.
To my parents, thank you for showing me the right road.
To my daughters, thank you for showing me how to love.
To Sensei, thank you for showing me how to be courageous.
To my uncle, thank you for being strong.
To my godmother, thank you for showing me
the importance of an education.
To my wife, thank you for pushing me forward.
To my gal, thank you for believing in me.
To Alisha, thank you for pointing me in the right direction.
To Michael, thank you for helping me heal.
To JoJo, thank you for caring about me.
To my brothers, thank you guys for the fun times.
To my partner, thank you for being understanding.
To my neighbors, thank you all for listening.
To humanity, thank you for your time.

Today Is the Day I Choose to Be Free

by Patricia Ann Klocko

Today is the day
I choose to be free
I may be burdened
And bound
I may be tied
My hands on my back
But for me
My day
My choice
I choose to be free
I am free to show the love
To those who do not know
The meaning of its truth
The love always within you
And always within me
I am free to love as I
Love to be free
I have built this wall of anger
You see
Was strong and bold
As I let it fold
The pieces of shame and regret
Lay worthless at my feet

February 11, 2017

Contents

Foreword

by Joe Mirenda

Luis and I met twenty-five years ago through a mutual friend. He was just finishing his tenure as a prosecutor for the district attorney's office and was about to embark on a new endeavor as a defense attorney at one of the most prominent criminal defense law firms on the West Coast. On the other hand, I was just your average, run-of-the-mill, working-class stiff, fresh off a broken marriage and looking for a place to hole up until I got my life back on track. Even though Luis barely knew me, he trusted his instincts and invited me to stay with him at the home he had just had built on the outskirts of Las Vegas. I'll never forget the first night I spent there. Luis put his hand on my shoulder, looked me in the eye, and said, "You're welcome to stay here as long as you want or for as long as you need." To someone picking up the pieces of their life and starting over again, no kinder words could have been spoken. When the Dalai Lama said, "Generosity is the most natural outward expression of an inner attitude of compassion and loving-kindness," he was speaking of Luis J. Rojas.

It was easy to see even way back then, long before he wrote the first page of *The Answer Is Love*, that for Luis, *love* truly was the answer.

Whether it was over dinner or a cold beer or when he was trying to teach me the finer points of chess, Luis would sometimes confide in me and share some of the more troubling cases he was working on. He'd always start out with, "I had to prosecute this poor kid today," or "I had to file a case against someone who never had a shot at life and it breaks my heart."

Now, don't get me wrong; if you flagrantly broke the law, Luis would drop the hammer on you in a heartbeat. He took his duties as a district attorney to heart and understood that he had a responsibility to keep the citizens of Las Vegas safe. But he also realized the future of the accused and their family hung in the balance, and if it was warranted, he'd ask the court to impose a lighter sentence on a deserving soul. One time, a judge asked Luis why the DA's office had agreed to a plea deal that included a lighter sentence for a defendant. Luis responded, "Your Honor, justice is supposed to be just, and sometimes showing *love* and compassion during a criminal proceeding is the right thing to do."

Like all of us, Luis has had his share of highs and lows. Because of his tremendous success as a criminal defense attorney, he was able to accumulate vast wealth. That wealth afforded him the opportunity to live a lifestyle that most of us could only dream of. Yet, despite that wealth, Luis never forgot his roots, and more importantly, his modest upbringing. Luis always considered his success a blessing. He would work tirelessly behind the scenes, personally counseling some of his clients, and in some cases, giving financial aid to those who had fallen on hard times. But beyond the achievements and accolades, Luis was hiding a dark secret that no success, notoriety, or wealth could quell, and it would plunge him into a recurring cycle of self-destructive behavior.

This book tells that story and so much more. Enjoy!

Joe Mirenda
Writer and Entrepreneur

Preface

What Is *Love?*

As humans, we consistently experience significant pain and suffering throughout our lives. In fact, great teachers, observing this reality we call *life*, have stated that the only constant during any particular lifetime is suffering. We not only experience suffering almost daily, but we hear about it over and over. We hear of sad events from strangers, acquaintances, and those we either work with or occasionally run across. Sometimes, when we hear of someone's good fortune, we quietly say to ourselves, "It couldn't have happened to a better person" or "I'm glad he got his." Other times, when calamities happen, we lament and cry because they happened to family members, friends, or even ourselves. Yet, typically today, we hear people say, "Everything happens for a reason." The question is why does suffering happen, and how does it serve a purpose in our lives? The answer is *Love.*

Love is seen by many people as a mystical concept used by the weak to justify their laziness. *Love* is also seen by much of our population as an antiquated concept that plays no part in modern society and is truly considered a sign of weakness. *Love* is considered by most individuals working in government as an ineffective tool against criminals, terrorists, and societal problems. Yet, we all have one common thread: We crave *Love* from the time of our birth to the time of our death. We all hurt when we don't receive *Love*, and we may panic if we think we will not find *Love* during our lifetime.

To understand the concept of *Love*, we must first start at the beginning. What is it exactly? How does it serve a purpose in our lives? Does it truly exist? Do we truly need it? What happens without *Love?* Last, where will *Love* take us?

As an American, a husband, a father, an attorney, and a former criminal prosecutor, I will share in this book some concepts about *Love* and some experiences from my life in an attempt to explain *Love.* I will identify what I originally understood *Love* to be and what presently *Love* is to me. I will also touch upon the absence of *Love* and what can occur due to the absence of *Love* in a person's life. Lastly, I will attempt to share with you how *Love* changes lives. I have actually seen *Love* at work, and I can tell you *Love* is real. I have discovered how encompassing *Love* is throughout our whole lifetime. It is the most powerful force on Earth.

I invite you to take this journey with me and discover more about how *Love* can change your life.

"Each according to the dictates of his own conscience."

— Norman Rockwell

Suggested listening: *I'd Like to Teach the World to Sing* by The New Seekers

Introduction

White-Haired Lady

"Love is more than a word; it is an emotion, an energy, and a feeling that creates a healing vibration to make your heart sing."

— Dr. Michael Gross

When I was young, I could not understand how I could get past the Pearly Gates and be admitted into my perceived version of heaven with all my sins and all my faults. Thus, began my search for the truth. But the search was long, never-ending in fact, as I looked everywhere for the solutions to this intricate puzzle we call life. For years, it seemed that the pieces of the puzzle were out of place and did not fit my reality. Under the mandates of my chosen life, I continued to grow and question my own existence. Then one day, the Universe showed me what was to come.

In 2001, shortly after getting married, I was out with my wife Edna (not her real name) at a local casino. We came across a fortune teller who had a small booth between the bathrooms and was offering palm and card readings for a small fee. Although I refused the reading, I convinced Edna to sit down and have her future read. After Edna was done, we headed home.

During the drive home, Edna explained that the fortune teller was very polite and informative. She had told Edna she would have a long life, but there was a very special time coming that would begin with the appearance of a "white-haired lady." When Edna asked who the "white-haired lady" was, the fortune teller said she would be an older woman with white hair down to the middle of her back who would approach Edna with a very special message. The fortune teller then told Edna to listen to the message because it would be life-changing. Edna assured the fortune teller she would keep her eyes and ears open for the "white-haired lady." Then, like any young couple, we took the message and stored it away in our minds.

In 2009, I was contacted by an unknown individual regarding a person who had been stopped by the police in Pioche, Nevada, for speeding. When the Nevada highway patrolman searched the bed of the truck, they found 483 pounds of neatly packaged and dry-sealed bags of marijuana under a tarp. I quoted my usual fee to the unknown individual. The case was approximately 200 miles north of Las Vegas, Nevada, in a small country town, so I said I would drive there to visit the defendant once I was retained. They paid the retainer that evening, and the next day, I was off in my Porsche to visit my new client.

When I got to the Lincoln County courthouse, I recognized an older gentleman, I'll call Sam, who was the county prosecuting attorney. Sam was waiting for me on the courthouse steps. When I pulled into the parking lot, he said, "Well, it looks like they hired a gun to come up from Las Vegas."

Sam was a former deputy public defender with whom I had a contentious relationship. He walked up to my car and said, "I'm the new county district attorney and this is the biggest drug case we've had in twenty years." Sam informed me my client was going to prison for possession and transportation with intent.

If I had a dollar for ever prosecutor who told me my client was going to prison when the client did not, I would be a rich man. Anyway, the case rolled on and my client did not go to prison. Although he did six months in the city jail, he really enjoyed the small-town hospitality and hot meals. He could come and go as he pleased while in jail, as long as he was in his jail cell before sunset. Throughout the day, he assisted the farmers in the fields. Believe it or not, my client ended up moving to this town after he served his sentence, and he lives there to this day.

On the last day of the case, Sam and I went to lunch before I was to head back to Las Vegas for good. While we were eating, Sam asked, "Do you know what university I graduated from?" He told me he went to Notre Dame University where he had earned a bachelor's degree in theology. He stayed on at Notre Dame to earn a master's in theology. I was incredibly impressed.

Sam then asked a question I will never forget.

"How are you doing in your heart and soul?"

I didn't know how to respond.

Sam suggested I read a book published in 1926 by Paramhansa Yogananda titled *The Autobiography of a Yogi*. After discussing some of the book's intricacies, Sam handed me his copy and said, "Good luck."

When I got home, I intensely began reading. I finished the book quickly, and a few days later, my life started to change as I began to follow the book's advice by meditating and quieting my mind. Interestingly enough, the more I quieted my mind, the more I heard.

Then it happened. I met Edna at a local casino for breakfast. While we were waiting, an elderly woman with long white hair down to the middle of her back approached our table and said, "I'm sorry to interrupt, but I have a message for you."

When I asked what it was, she said, "A great spiritual master asked me earlier today to meet you here to tell you he would like to get to know you a little better, and if you develop a personal relationship with him, you will change the lives of millions of people."

Then she left.

A few days later, I began writing this book.

Throughout this book there are messages sent to me by the Universe to include for my reader. These messages were written down exactly as I was told them by the Universe. They were not doctored or manipulated by me in any way. My intention in including these messages is to raise the reader's consciousness and vibration. Further, at the end of every chapter, I have suggested a song for you to listen to. I would respectfully suggest you read a chapter a day, when permitted by your schedule, and then listen to the song suggested along with viewing the lyrics for that particular song. Through this method, you may find hidden messages from the Universe.

Just like each picture can tell a complete story, so can a song. More importantly, I believe each song suggested captures the vibration of both the book and the chapter. The song will help raise your vibration to one that will open up both your conscious and subconscious minds to the material presented herein. So, here we go! Buckle up for the ride because it is an intense rollercoaster of a story.

"Every action has an equal and an opposite reaction."

— Isaac Newton

Suggested listening: *All You Need Is Love* by The Beatles

Chapter 1

Love

"Love is the heartbeat of all life."

— Paramhansa Yogananda

As I headed out of the house, I could not get the smell of a nice cup of coffee out of my mind. So after mentally planning my route for downtown, I started picturing a nice tall latte with one raw sugar. The imagined aroma was driving me crazy since I drink a lot of coffee. So, as I drove hastily toward my favorite coffee joint, I realized my coffee stop would make me late for my morning appointment.

While en route, I texted my client to let her know I would be about twenty minutes late for our meeting. For me, mornings are hectic because I live twenty-seven miles from my law office in downtown Las Vegas. On an average day, it takes me thirty minutes to get to work. If there is an accident on the freeway, it takes closer to forty-five.

Yes, Las Vegas, Nevada. A fast town, made up of fast people, moving at light speed all day and all night. They move so fast they lose track of the time and the day. After riding the wave of party life for a few days, one could mistake sunrise for sunset and sunset for sunrise. For me, I work all day long and come out of hyperdrive after 5 p.m. Then the fun begins. That's the same for most professionals in this big city. Hotel employees are different. They work all day long, around the clock, day after day.

"What do I do?" you ask. Well, I am a criminal defense attorney in the crime capital of the world. For the last seventeen years, I have worked at one of the most powerful criminal defense firms in town. We represent boys, girls, ladies, men, judges, cops, prosecutors, criminals, and everyone in between. Prior to working at the firm, I worked at the district attorney's office as a deputy district attorney. I put many criminals away to protect society. Coming from a blue collar family, I left the district attorney's office because I wanted to make more money.

Living hard and practicing hard almost killed me, in more ways than one. They say those who work hard also play hard; for me, that was an understatement. Fortunately, I took what I had seen happen, what I had done, and what I saw unfolding as a life lesson. After practicing criminal law for twenty-two years in Vegas, I received an understanding of life and the Universe. I know it sounds crazy, but many Vegas stories end with someone jumping off a building onto the concrete street below. Other stories end with someone being driven out to the desert and never being heard from again. My story is quite different.

But let's get back to my morning. I was waiting in line to order my drink behind a few vehicles. Naturally, I was in a rush to get to work. As I rolled down my window, a young girl said, "Welcome to.... I would like to get something started for you to make your day happier." For the first time that morning, the thought of happiness entered my mind. I then ordered my drink and the young girl said, "It will be my pleasure to get that started for you immediately, sir." As I sat there, the word *Love* rang in my ears and in my head. So, instead of rolling up my window, I decided to keep my window down.

I don't know if you know, but Vegas is hot in the summer. No, not just hot—scorching hot. Daytime temperatures can reach up to 115 degrees Fahrenheit. Today was no different. It was really hot, but I could not feel the heat. I could only feel the *Love.*

While I was waiting for my coffee, I kept the window down to listen to this young lady interact with the other customers. Her happiness had caught my attention and changed my morning focus. As I listened to her, she made comments to the other drivers like "It is wonderful to see you again," "I can't wait till you taste what I made for you today," and "You're going to be real happy with this one." Her interactions were filled with positive service and energetic comments of goodwill and kindness.

As I overheard her conversations, I realized her happiness was genuine and real. Customers were joking with her and laughing, even while being in the hot Las Vegas sun. Then I rolled up to the pickup window. I looked in the window and saw a young girl, probably around eighteen, with a beautiful big smile. She looked at me and said, "I've got your drink ready, and I made this one especially for you." When she addressed me, she immediately made me feel special. She made me feel *Loved.*

She then asked how my day was going. I replied, "Wonderful, but even better now." I asked her how her day was going, and she replied,

"Great!" I was taken back by her direct and confident response. It showed no weakness and let me know exactly where she was at that time in her life. As I looked into her eyes, I could feel her sincerity and warmth. I asked her, "How old are you?" She replied that she was twenty. In her radiance, the Universe spoke to me.

The Universe speaks to us directly and through us to others constantly. You know what I'm speaking of. It usually happens when you are focused on a particular point and all of the commotion around you just kind of dies away. In this silence, all of a sudden, a powerful thought comes into your mind, ringing of truth and spoken with complete clarity. It typically involves an important point, answer, or comment that, usually, you were not even thinking about. Some of us listen, while most of us choose not to hear its words. To disconnect from the Universe, some of us go as far as using drugs and alcohol so we don't have to process such revelations. We are too caught up in our own conduct to allow any interference from anything or anyone.

Many of us believe that by listening, we create an internal struggle, which, in turn, would create self-doubt in ourselves and destroy our self-confidence. This "self-confidence" is essential in our present "dog eat dog world," where the slightest hint of weakness could result in great suffering for you and those you *Love.* Furthermore, who has time to consider all of those crazy thoughts that bombard our minds throughout the day?

I have learned that when the Universe speaks to you, it speaks clearly and without doubt. It happens when you are centered and at a peaceful place surrounded by *Love.* It usually speaks to me while I am taking my morning shower. After I get up, I usually read and then center myself through meditation. Then I get into the shower. I like my showers hot. The steam and the effects of the hot water hitting my body put me in a relaxed space, which allows me to connect with the Universe.

On this day, the Universe spoke loud and clear in the coffee shop drive-thru. As a result of the young female attendant's actions, I transcended to a peaceful place where I felt accepted and *Loved.* Simply, I was the center of her attention. I was in *Love.*

No, we did not run away together and live happily ever after. But I felt as if time and the scorching heat were not present. I felt an uninterrupted channel of communication existed between us that was not affected by the many annoying factors of our present existence. We were in a place outside of time and space. No, the feelings were not sexual in nature, but they were real and genuine at both an emotional and spiritual level.

I looked at her and said, "In the entire Universe, there is nothing more beautiful than a person who truly is in *Love.*" I then explained to her that throughout her life, many people would attempt to steal or extinguish her light of *Love.* I told her to fight for the *Love.*

We all know some people will try to lie and cheat you. They will befriend you only to get at you, and then they will steal from you, beat you, and leave you lying half-dead in the street. They will speak horribly about you behind your back and criticize your every move while telling you how wonderful you are.

As we continued our conversation, I told her she should protect her beautiful gift with all her might. She was startled by the energy her *Love* had generated. She smiled and said, "Thank you."

As I drove away, my insecurities immediately stepped in to fill the void left behind.

First, I thought, *Who are you to speak for the Universe*? Then, as an attorney, I said to myself, "You haven't seen the Universe; how can you make such a bold claim?" Then, I started with my deductive reasoning by thinking, *The birth of your child, the Grand Canyon, the oceans with their beautiful creatures are just as beautiful*. Followed by the thought, *Did I just make a fool of myself*? The answers came through loud and clear....

Message From The Universe:

> You are made of the same materials as the stars and planets. In your universal consciousness you carry with you the ability to know the universal truths. The truth has a distinct vibration and feeling. The birth of a child is grand, as are mountains, oceans, and stars, in the perspective of the glory of the Universe. There is nothing more beautiful in the Universe than to see another human being truly happy. This is to experience the vibration of love physically, emotionally, and spiritually. It was this love that created the Universe. You did not make a fool of yourself.

I was happy to finally understand the saying "Truth has a certain ring." See, for many years, I did not personally understand this concept. As a young law student, I was taught that statements were solely evaluated from a factual perspective. Now, I evaluate a statement far differently.

"Truth" resonates at a higher energy frequency in our world, leaving a specific vibrational feeling imprinted on our minds, bodies, and souls. Based on the vibrational imprint left by a statement or a message, we decide whether the statement is true or false. We then apply our own personal factual perspective of the statement to conclude whether it is true or false. Day in and day out, we are bombarded with statements for which we have no factual basis upon which to judge their veracity. These statements are evaluated based upon their vibrational frequency and their energy.

False statements create a different feeling at the lower end of the vibrational spectrum. How many times have you heard someone say something you immediately thought was untrue? You thought, *That's not right*, yet you had no independent information to reject or deny the assertion. Later, you found out it was actually untrue. You picked up on the person's vibration, and you picked up on the energy carried in their spoken words. Based upon your introspective analysis, you properly concluded that what they said was false.

Interestingly enough, parents can tell immediately when their child is not being truthful. They see and feel their child's vibrational frequency and energy when they're telling a lie. They also feel the energy in the child's words. Although the parent did not witness the child eating the cookie before dinner, the parent immediately knows if the child did so.

Unfortunately, sometimes we cannot discern the veracity of a statement. In giving another the benefit of the doubt, we choose to accept the statement as true. Yet, most of us, deep down inside, know true statements from false.

As I drove into the parking garage at work that day, I was at peace with the message I had just received. I felt happy about this newfound understanding of my existence.

My workday started with a call to an insurance adjuster for a personal injury case I was handling. I know it sounds intimidating if you're not a legal person, but just think of it as the typical wolf and shepherd dog relationship from the old cartoon. They like each other until they clock-in. If you think a criminal prosecutor can be tough, try a young insurance adjuster who just got hired and is trying to save the company money so they can keep their job and get a bonus at the end of the year.

Much to my surprise, the adjuster working on the case answered the phone immediately and asked how I was doing. I responded, "Wonderful," and explained to her how happy I was to have met a young woman working at a coffee shop who radiated *Love.* I explained how I was overcome by her courage to be so *openly happy.* I also commented on how many people in our society are *not happy.* I explained to the adjuster that I intentionally used the words "not happy" instead of "unhappy." To me an "unhappy person" is one in a state of frustration, extreme anxiety, anger, or sadness. A "not happy person" is a person who is just devoid of happiness, going through the motions necessary to exist, but not necessarily angry, frustrated, anxious, or sad. An example would be a person in the emotional state of boredom.

When I asked the insurance adjuster how she was doing, she said, "I'm okay." I said, "Just okay?" and then used the courage I had just received from my newfound *Love* experience to say, "Come on; it's a beautiful day out there. Think of how many new experiences we both are going to have today!" She laughed and said, "You seem to be in a great mood." I said, "I am." Now, I was talking the language of the Universe. Then I used my newfound courage to ask the adjuster, "Are you happy today?"

Immediately, a voice inside of me responded, "How dare you ask her that question! That is none of your business!" I feared the insurance adjuster would say, "Who do you think you are to ask me such a question?" or "This is a professional conversation regarding a civil matter, so my personal emotional state is none of your concern."

What I had not counted on was that my happiness had opened the door and given this insurance adjuster the courage to explore her own happiness. She replied, "That is tough to answer. How do you define being happy?" All of a sudden, the Universe spoke through me again....

Message From The Universe:

Love is a state of being. It comes from knowing your place in the Universe and being at peace with the equality of all things. It is through this understanding of equality that the soul becomes satisfied and can resonate happiness through the self and onto others. This vibrational resonance is called love. Love is the law of the Universe. Love is always present in the space of now. As the basic and main building block to our existence, it is the glue that keeps this reality together. It is incredibly underestimated, but it is highly contagious to human beings if allowed to develop. In the alternative, the ego fights against equality through judgment, therefore spawning prosecution, persecution, and competition between human beings.

As I took a second to soak this in, I acknowledged that, although the insurance adjuster and I were adversaries, we could both enjoy the young woman's happiness and possibly explore the subject of *Love.* Her next statement blew me away. She said, "I wish I was happier, but when I look around and see all the sadness, all the senseless violence, and all the hate, it makes me feel like we're doomed."

I appreciated the adjuster's courage in discussing this sensitive topic openly with a total stranger, so I responded, "I see the news about violence and hate. It makes me sad, but I can tap into *Love*, knowing there are millions upon millions of acts of kindness across the world every day." I explained these acts are done by wonderful people with great hearts, not for their own benefit, but for the benefit of the entire Universe. I said, "Their sole purpose is to make others happy."

She said, "You're right. I wish more people understood that."

Then we pleasantly discussed the facts and issues of the case. No, I did not get a great settlement from her. No, I didn't get everything I wanted from her company, but from our conversation, I got much more. I learned another person was concerned for my happiness and for the world's.

She gained an understanding that *Love* resonates through all of us onto others. It moves through them and throughout our respective societies, which eventually leads to *Love* permeating our entire planet. She also saw I was interested in her happiness as a person. Our conversation ended with wishing each other a very "good morning."

We agreed the world needed more people who displayed *Love* openly.

Every day, we are blessed. Some of us start our day early and some start late. Either way, every day has a beginning. Similarly, every day has an ending. What happens in between those two very important events dictates how our day goes.

Many of us start our day in a state of panic. We jump out of bed and rush to the shower. We take a shower as quickly as we can, rushing to get ready for work. Once we are ready, we run out of our homes and into our cars, driving off as quickly as possible, hoping we can get to work on time. On the way, our minds are flooded with tasks that must be completed. Often, we even begin taking care of business while driving. Texting, calling, and emailing from our cars is normal in today's fast-paced world.

Others start their days before the rest of their family awakens. Whether a mother or a father, parents typically have an internal clock getting them up in the morning. Most parents would say their internal clock is set around their children getting up and their partners getting to work. It is essential to these parents and partners that things are prepared and ready for the family so they can get a good start on their "100-yard-dash day," as so many of us today call life. Try to talk to a parent at 6 a.m. and you will probably hear, "Not now. I'm running late!"

Still other people wake up and run to the shower to get ready for school or work. Whether class starts at eight or you have to clock in by noon, there is always a mad dash to make it on time. Some of us go so far as to eliminate taking a shower just to sleep for an extra few minutes. Whether we have to review material for class or have to stop at the gas station, we are all running late for a very important date.

Inevitably, we all end up in traffic. This can mean traffic literally, as it does for those of us who end up on the actual freeway. But it can also mean traffic figuratively, as in the traffic of thoughts we constantly entertain. I wish I could tell you our present-day freeways are long roads that allow us to travel safely to our destination while contemplating the meaning of life. Unfortunately, for most of us, getting on the freeway is either like sitting in the parking lot or being in the Grand Prix. Regardless, the clock is ticking and work, school, or class all start soon. Yet, I'm sitting there not moving or stressing out about driving the speed of light and possibly hitting another vehicle, which is also going the speed of light. What is the boss going to say? How is my teacher going to react? Am I going to get fired? Will I get an incomplete?

The stress, fear, frustration, and anxiety build and build. Once you get to your destination, you are a ticking time bomb ready to explode. At that moment, happiness is replaced with anxiety, frustration, and being short-tempered. *Love* no longer resonates from the self but is replaced by fear. This fear is then distributed to others, who can then feel your unhappy vibrations. Your fear has a profound effect on those around you.

Typically, fear creates stress, which is recognized and processed by both your conscious and subconscious mind and the minds of others. We vacillate so quickly from the past (what did I do that made me so late) to the future (what is going to happen) that we never stop for a second to live in the now. *Love* exists in the present and opens the door for positive connections to the Universe and your neighbor.

People like the young barista see life for what it truly is. Life is simple. Life is all about *Love.* People can argue for hours about where you go after you die. This book is not intended to be a spiritual debate on the afterlife, but for certain, what we have is the here and now. What that young woman understood is that what truly matters is *Love*—both her moments of *Love* and other people's moments of *Love.* Through this connection of *Love,* your true self is recognized and understood.

That young woman understood that *Love* can connect you to others at a high vibrational frequency. This high frequency is void of the mundane static present in our normal existence. She understood that once the customer felt her *Love* through her appreciation and kindness, they would become more *Loving,* which would cause them to be kinder and to appreciate others. And she understood that through this combined *Love,* the world would begin to accept others and cultivate peace and happiness.

What interacting with that young barista taught me was that, upon waking up in the morning, my main focus should not be on where am I headed or my first daily task. My main focus upon waking should be seeing life with a *Loving* state of mind.

I know we all have problems, but we must understand that any bad situation could be worse. Take a second to think about what is making you so unhappy and just imagine how the situation could be made worse. This simple exercise will give you a proper perspective and allow you to appreciate your present situation.

For example, if you are reading this, you must be alive. I'm sure you're saying to yourself "duh." But don't forget many people around the world will not have the opportunity to read this book or anything else because they died yesterday. Whether by accident, by another's hand, or just natural causes, they do not have the opportunity you have today. So cherish it. Make the most of the experiences you will have today!

Today, you will touch many lives, not only through interactions with friends and family but through interactions with other individuals you encounter throughout your day. You will speak and communicate with others at the coffee shop, the restaurant, the convenience store, and the gas station.

If we take it upon ourselves to make these interactions pleasurable and have the courage to exhibit our *Love* for others, then this world would move away from anger, judgment, frustration, anxiety, and fear—all of which are common denominators for thoughts of the past and thoughts of the future.

Seeing your *Love* can make others smile and forget about their problems. Your *Love* can be contagious and spread like wildfire to others, who then can pass it on through their happiness. Your *Love* can provide others with the courage and strength to be happy and display their *Love* openly. Your *Love* allows you to see both the freeway and the workplace through rose-colored glasses, thereby helping you appreciate both. Your *Love* allows for understanding between friends, families, and even adversaries. It encourages you to smile and say, "Today I choose *Love*." It creates the foundation for your existence in the present.

The answer truly is *Love.*

"To experience true love is to see the reality behind every action and occurrence and to understand how each relates to you as the ultimate participant."

Suggested listening: *Love Is the Answer* by England Dan and John Ford Coley

Chapter 2

Accepting Love

"Love is the absence of judgment."

— Dalai Lama XIV

Living in Las Vegas has been wonderful. I have seen and experienced so many different and amazing things in this beautiful city. Wow, I'm as old as some trees. Especially some trees in my yard. Although Las Vegas is a newer city, Clark County is the eighth largest county in the United States. When I graduated from high school, the population of the entire county was 250,000. Today, it is nearly ten times that.

I have truly enjoyed my life in this beautiful city. During my time here, I have heard Las Vegas called many different names—Party Town USA, Sin City, etc. But I have called it home since I was a baby.

What was growing up in Las Vegas like? It was wonderful, but it was very hot. My father worked in the gaming industry as a casino worker, which provided a good living. We were a typical American family with two kids. My father's work schedule, without exception, was 3:30 p.m. to 2:00 a.m., Tuesday through Saturday. He had Sunday and Monday off.

On my father's days off, we did family things away from the Las Vegas strip. The Las Vegas strip was not for children, and it was too much like work for my dad to go visit. Like so many families in the 1970s, most of my contact growing up was with one parent since the other parent worked to pay the bills.

For the majority of my childhood, my mother was a stay-at-home mom who spent her time religiously cooking and cleaning. My mother never took any time for herself, spending her days taking care of her family. Our home was spotless, and the food was out of this world.

My mother can cook all types of food. Over the years, she became a phenomenal cook. Even today, anyone who tastes her food says it is the best. One reason is she only uses the freshest ingredients and finest meats. The other reason is she is so patient in the kitchen. Once you have a bite of one of her many fabulous dishes, you can't get enough.

We were a typical middle class American family, with my parents saving all their pennies for our private schools and family vacations. Unlike myself, my parents do not drink or party. They are straightforward conservatives who believe there are consequences for each and every action. They are stringent church-goers, who never took much time for themselves. Overall, my parents are wonderful people who did the best they could with the information they had learned and experienced. Anyone looking in from the outside would have thought everything about our lives was just wonderful. But looks can be very deceiving. Unfortunately, when I was young, in our home there was a problem.

My mother is a very proud woman, one who is extremely proud of her family and extremely critical of everything else. She is a beautiful woman with some formal education. She protects her family from the world like a lioness. Her sole mission was to make her family and her children successful in this new country. There was no horse-play with her; her function as a mother was to tell you what your problem was so you could correct your behavior. I can undoubtedly say my mother was the driving force behind the person I am today. For that, I will always be grateful.

We lived in a four-bedroom home with a gorgeous swimming pool. As a young child, I spent many summer hours playing "Marco Polo" and "Shark and Minnows" in the pool until the late evening. It was a picture-perfect home for a picture-perfect family—except for one dirty little secret.

I had a beautiful bedroom as a child. I had a comfortable, large bed, beautiful furniture, a solid wood desk, and more toys than I knew what to do with. At a very young age, I was responsible for making my bed first thing in the morning. I was also responsible for keeping my bedroom neat and tidy. Anyone who visited us and saw my room was impressed by how immaculate it looked. But inside my bedroom, hidden underneath my sheets, in my bed, was a dirty little secret. I was a *bedwetter*.

Regardless of what people may think or say, bedwetting is a significant experience. Presently, it is estimated that 5 to 7 million children in the United States wet their beds. Some parents see this as deviant behavior that must be corrected for their child to fit in and have a chance in society.

Unfortunately, this experience is often painful, leaving the child with deep psychological scars. The child then buries those feelings deep inside. In psychology, this behavior is known as repression. Yet the answer to stopping this repetitive, destructive pain and suffering is right in front of us. *Love* is the answer.

"Repression" is defined in medical terms as:

> [A]n unconscious defense mechanism whereby unacceptable thoughts, feelings, ideas, impulses, or memories, especially those concerning some traumatic past event, are pushed from the consciousness because of the painful guilt association or disagreeable content and are submerged in the unconscious, where they remain dormant but operant and dynamic. Such emotional conflicts are the source of anxiety that may lead to any of the anxiety disorders.[1]

Any negative experience, when repressed, can create destructive thoughts and behaviors until it is truly addressed. My goal here is to bring some *Love* to the millions of people who find themselves in this difficult experience and help them through it. Hopefully, they can use some of my suggestions to work through their painful experience and alleviate some of their pain and suffering. Once we have worked through the experience, we can move through the pain and suffering and enter a state of peace and equality with others.

How do we do this? First, we must look at the experience and examine how the pain was created. Then, we must find a way to rectify the hurt and damage. I would like to offer my personal childhood

---

1. *Mosby's Dictionary, Medical Nursing, and Allied Health.* 3rd ed. 1990.

experience with wetting the bed as one example. Bedwetting happens millions of times a night to children of all ages all around the world. To better understand the dynamics of this experience, let's take a close look at my bedwetting.

Bedwetting is terrifying to a child and can be just as devastating to their parents. Can you imagine waking up in the middle of the night, or in the early morning, feeling wet all over? This is no pool or shower wetness. It is an uncomfortable and smelly wetness that makes you want to run and hide from everything and everyone. When you are alone, you cry because you let your parents down. You can't figure out what you did wrong since your only crime was sleeping. Yet, when you wake up, you feel like you did something very bad. You feel alone, and you feel afraid.

You don't dare spend the night at a friend's home. Even worse, if a friend finds out you are a "bedwetter," neighbors and your classmates may uncover your shameful secret. Then the whole town will know. This is all terrifying to a child.

You feel as if you will most certainly lose your friends if it becomes known you are a bedwetter. You believe everyone will make fun of you. It is a sad and lonely world for the bedwetter. You feel you are somehow flawed and different from other kids. You feel inferior and isolated, seeing yourself on an island.

I remember one night in particular when I was about ten. My little brother Jed had had a nightmare and secretly snuck into my room. I was ecstatic to have someone in my room, no less in my bed, for the night. Sadly, I was alone in my bed as a child 100 percent of the time because of my problem. That night, Jed and I stayed as quiet as possible to avoid alerting our parents.

At about 4 a.m., Jed woke up and started crying loudly. Everything happened so fast! The lights were turned on abruptly. My poor little brother was wet from head to toe and so was my bedding and mattress. I had wet the bed again.

My parents were furious because they had to change two kids out of their dirty pajamas. They also had to change the bed sheets and put us back to sleep. Not a task to envy for anyone at 4 a.m. I felt terrible about the whole ordeal. I apologized over and over again.

I was mortified by this uncontrollable accident. I now believe my bedwetting was caused by my deep-sleep patterns and stress. The wounds of my bedwetting run so deep, even today, that just speaking of them causes some fear. My saving grace has been in accepting the experience and the reactions of those involved.

Could you imagine if, after peeing your bed, your parents said you were bad because you wet your bed? As a child, you go to school and do your best to make your parents proud. After school, you go home and do your homework to the best of your ability to make your parents happy. After you finish your homework, you play for a while, and then you start getting ready for bed. You put on your pajamas, brush your teeth, and pray just like any good kid. Then you simply go to sleep to rest your growing body. It should be a peaceful time of rest and rejuvenation.

Instead, you are terrified of going to sleep. Sometimes, you try to stay up all night just so you don't pee the bed and disappoint your parents. You hope that by some miracle, you won't pee the bed and your parents will show you the *Love* you so much crave.

Suddenly, you are awakened by the wetness. You run to your parents for help, and they start yelling at you. They tell you that you are bad because you had an accident. They tell you this is bad behavior and it needs to stop. You sit there wondering how it happened again. You pray it never happens again.

All you're really praying for is acceptance.

Message From The Universe:

> Acceptance is love in motion. Through acceptance, you acknowledge the circumstances and those involved, but you do not judge either the participants or the events. By accepting the event in its entirety, you see how the event serves you and how the event serves in the growth of all involved. Everything is all good for everyone!

You see, it is human nature for parents to be mad that they had to get up in the middle of the night to change their child's sheets. Then this anger is multiplied by the frustration of having to wash the sheets again and again. Then hate jumps into the equation, as they think, *I hate that my child pees the bed.*

Compounding the problem, the child internalizes the fear by asking, "What if this never stops?" The typical reaction is for the parent to turn to the great demoralizer—guilt.

Message From The Universe:

> Guilt is an emotional response caused by fear. Specifically, it is the fear of being unloved, unworthy, or less than others. It is a fear-driven response in which you believe you are not acceptable because of your behavior, your thoughts, your condition, or your consequences. Within this suspected flaw, you believe you are no longer equal to the rest of humanity. When guilt is internalized, it lowers your vibrational state. It is an illusion and not recognized by the Universe. Unfortunately, the person imposing the guilt generally believes they are helping or enlightening you. You must protect yourself from guilt!

In dealing with any perceived problem, guilt usually turns the problem, whether big or small, into a monumental wrong. Guilt does this by undermining you, thereby devastating your self-confidence. Without self-confidence, you do not have the courage to dissect the experience and find the benefits.

See, my bedwetting was perceived by my family as a wrong I needed to correct so I could be "perfect." Only by achieving this imagined perfection would I have a chance in the world. In my parents' minds, anything less than perfect was unacceptable. Since my problem was their problem, they attempted to correct my behavior by using guilt.

Using guilt to solve my issue was like trying to give a person a haircut with a chainsaw. The hair would be cut off, but there sure would be a lot of scars left behind. That person is then left to deal with those scars for the rest of their life. Some people accept the pain caused by the experience and move on. Others choose to hold on to the pain until one day they are ready to move through the experience. Regardless of who you are or where you come from, we all deal with the pain and suffering caused by our negative experiences.

Let's take a moment to identify the sources of our suffering and pain. We all cope differently with pain and suffering, depending on our life experiences. Look deep inside and follow the path backwards from the guilt to the experiences that caused it. Once we begin to examine that path, we begin to see the signs of how our guilt came to be.

Message From The Universe:

> Remember you are a rightful member of this great and vast Universe. Regardless of how you were created, you are here now. Therefore, it is your birthright to experience all the choices you manifest. Specifically, you have the right to experience all the possible outcomes from the choices you make. But I must warn you, be careful because dire consequences can stem directly from your choices. See, you have the right to make the choices, but when you do, you own the decision and have earned the consequences. Regardless of the outcomes, every experience serves the universal purpose of enlightenment. Love is the law of the Universe.

In examining this road, you will see whether the guilt comes from within or was imposed by others. Only then can you examine the choices that formed each individual experience. This will help you determine which choices you would make again and which you wouldn't. Unfortunately, guilt is used so often that we feel guilty about things we have no control over, like bedwetting.

Put your guilt aside for a second. Let's focus on the real and great you. We are all stardust. The compounds of iron and calcium that comprise a major portion of our body are not organic in nature but derived from the explosion of a star.

Now, that you remember your greatness, let's take the first step toward healing by applying *Love* to eradicate guilt. Like so many children, I felt guilt because of my bedwetting issue. But let's look to see if we can find any *Love* in my bedwetting experience. Specifically, let's look for a place where peace and equality reside.

The reality is that no child is born with the ability to control their bladder. In fact, researchers have discovered that the nerves that control the bladder are controlled by the brain and are slow to mature. As time goes by, a child's brain fully develops, and so does their ability to control urination. Then one day, as if by magic, they become fully potty trained.[2]

What we know is that most of us experience bedwetting at some point. Whether we are too young or too old to control our bladder, it happens to the majority of us during our lifetimes. So, in actuality, bedwetting is not anomalous and/or deviant behavior; it is a human experience most of us go through.

Let's continue by injecting *Love* into my bedwetting experience. Now that we know most of us will wet the bed at some point, we need to ask, "What's the big deal with wetting the bed?" The honest

2. MayoClinic.Org/Diseases-Conditions/Bedwetting-causes. October 26, 2017.

answer is it is *not* a big deal. No one dies or drowns from bedwetting. So, either buy the right size diapers for the individual—they make them in all sizes and for all ages—or get up and change the sheets. Simple enough.

Humans often make a big deal out of nothing. We sensationalize what people say, and then we turn around and sensationalize what they didn't say. Yes, lots of things are a big deal, but they are not usually the things we are actually talking about.

I believe hurting another person is a big deal. I believe breaking a person's heart is a big deal. I believe killing a person's self-confidence is a big deal. However, the car a superstar drove to the awards ceremony or the dress a superstar wore to receive an award I do not believe are big deals.

My father once told me, "Don't make a big deal out of things that aren't a big deal." Of course, that didn't mean much to me when he said it, but now it means a lot. In thinking bedwetting is no big deal, and in knowing all of us do it, a person may come to accept the experience. This includes accepting the actions and behavior of those involved in the experience.

I am sure you handle much more difficult issues daily. The truth is the frustration and anxiety typical in the bedwetting paradigm is not only from the child, but is compounded immensely by the parents' reaction to the event. Since the child is constantly learning from the parents, if the parents have a negative reaction, the child will feel guilt, which will cause pain and suffering. This incredibly stressful environment stems directly from the experience. This scenario of compounding guilt is present in all life experiences.

Let me share how this situation worked for me. It will take you full circle. Like I said earlier, life is a wonderful experience. Sometimes, life blesses you with the same experience again to help you grow. I now have two children. Guess what? One of my children also wets the bed.

One particular evening when my daughter Sue was about five, she asked to sleep in my bed. I really didn't have an issue with that, but I immediately recognized that my child was checking out my attitude and feelings. I said, "Of course, it would be my pleasure to have you sleep with me." From my own personal experience, I recognized the importance of the coming night and the following morning.

I set up a good game plan so we didn't have to worry about the mattress. I opened up a trash bag and placed it in my bed under the sheets while Sue was taking a shower and getting ready for bed. I also had her wear older children's diapers so if an accident happened, the effects would be minimal. Then we both fell asleep like two rocks. We didn't get up once that night to go to the bathroom.

The next morning, I felt wetness. Sue had urinated through the diapers, through the garbage bag, and onto the bed. Although, I had never said one thing about my bedwetting issue, when I woke up, Sue was curled into a ball in the corner of my bed. She was terrified. Sue was about to start crying and began to apologize.

At that moment, I was transported through time and space to my childhood.

I could feel Sue's pain and suffering through my own bedwetting experiences. I relived every single time I had urinated in the bed, and I thought of all the sad memories. It is crazy, but time slowed down, as if the whole Universe were listening to what I was going to say next. I thought, *Isn't this just bizarre*? I wondered, *Do I use guilt, the great demoralizer? Do I act like it didn't happen? What do I do?*

Message From The Universe:

The answer is love.

I turned to Sue, and said, "It's no big deal."

My beautiful child was shocked. See, children are not only very intuitive, but they often assume the worst in stressful situations. I don't know if it's a learned behavior or part of nature's defense mechanisms. All I know is my daughter was sitting there terrified, not knowing what would happen next.

As I walked around the bed, I said to Sue, "When I was your age, I had an accident and peed all over Uncle Jed one night when he was sleeping in my bed."

Her eyes perked up, and she said, "Really, Daddo?"

I then sat down on the bed and said, "I also wet the bed when I was little."

Sue was shocked by my candor. I told her I had peed the bed until I was twelve. I also said I had peed the bed so many times when I was young that my parents lost count. A smile spread across Sue's face, and I could see the fear dissipating. I hugged her and said, "It wasn't a big deal when I peed my bed, and it isn't a big deal that you peed this bed."

Looking back, I realize that saying it wasn't a big deal with a true heart allowed me to accept my own bedwetting experience for the first time. Can you believe I finally did it? It took me until I was forty-six years old to truly accept that particular experience. I had seen the parity in our individual experiences, as if Sue and I were both going through the same experience almost simultaneously. When it happened, I was finally at peace with myself and all those with whom I shared my bedwetting experience.

With a full heart and a new perspective, I said, "I *Love* you."

"I *Love* you too, Dad," Sue said.

After I accepted the experience, I took the opportunity to apply some positive reinforcement. I said, "Well, you see, I got potty trained, and when the time is right, so will you." Sue laughed, jumped off the bed, and ran off to wash up. I grabbed the dirty sheets and put them in the washing machine. Once we cleaned up, we had a wonderful breakfast. We never spoke of that experience again, yet it was monumental for us both.

Sue knew her father truly believed that wetting the bed was no big deal, which made her also believe it was no big deal. My daughter also understood that wetting the bed happens to other children and recognized that when the time was right, the bedwetting would stop. Sue understood as well that bedwetting is sometimes part of life and it does not make someone a bad person. I know that, through my acceptance, I had given her valuable information that allowed her, too, to accept the experience. Not long after, Sue was fully potty trained.

For me, the importance of that moment was even greater. By accepting my bedwetting experience and helping with my daughter's bedwetting experience, I conquered my pain and suffering from this particular issue. I also ended a long cycle of "hereditary pain."

Message From The Universe:

Hereditary pain is the pain inherited from generation to generation. It is pain caused by some form of perceived guilt, which is internalized over the years in the subconscious mind. Adults transfer the guilt to their children or relatives when a similar experience arises. At that moment, the pain and suffering of many generations can be transposed onto a child or relative through guilt. This guilt then makes the person feel unloved, unworthy, and lesser than.

The pain and suffering caused by a recurring experience can be multiplied exponentially on a child depending on the severity of the response. So, how do you conquer this hereditary pain? *Love* again is the answer.

In Sue's experience with wetting the bed, I could have said, "Oh no!" and I could have thought, *Here we go again!* Then I could have lashed out at Sue for "her behavior." I could have allowed frustration, anxiety, and fear to seep out of me by responding with anger. I could have lied to her and said, "I never peed my bed!"

All of these responses would have made Sue feel unworthy and less than. As a result, my daughter could have lost her sense of equality.

That could have manifested into feelings of guilt during her adolescent years. I would have pushed the pain I felt from my bedwetting experience onto her and scarred her psyche for many years to come.

What does a child do once scarred? They hide the pain deep inside until they have enough courage to cope with the issue. Sadly, such reactions from parents disrupt the child's natural vibration of *Love* and introduce guilt and hereditary pain. If you do react badly, the key is to recognize what you have done and try to neutralize the negative effects of your actions.

Let's start to heal from the guilt and hereditary pain caused by all of our diverse and difficult experiences. Find the strength and courage to exercise patience, acceptance, and understanding under all circumstances.

Once again, *Love* is the answer.

> "Every morning is a symbol of rebirth of our life, so forget all yesterday's bad moments and make today the most beautiful day of your life."
>
> — Shakyamuni Buddha

Suggested listening: *Everybody Hurts* by R.E.M.

Chapter 3

Love You

"I have found the paradox, that if you love until it hurts, there can be no more hurt, only more love."

— Mother Teresa

I want to start this chapter by telling you that I *Love* you.

These refreshing words are too often overlooked. While many feel the warm vibration of these beautiful words, some feel they are antiquated. Many people really don't feel comfortable with these words. All our reactions are understandable because each relates directly to our childhood.

Before we travel back in time, I must share something that just happened the other day. First, I have two beautiful daughters, Sue and Maggie, who are the loves of my life. These beautiful human beings are not perfect—they have the same problems all children have. One day, I went downstairs to talk to Sue, who was twelve at the time. She was on her cell phone—in classic juvenile behavior, she is always on her cell phone watching videos, playing games, or talking to friends.

I wanted to talk to her about something I felt was important, but Sue just wouldn't get off the phone. I tapped her shoulder and asked her to get off the phone. She said, "No," which, of course, frustrated me. I asked her again to get off the phone, which frustrated her.

What happened next was out of character for both of us.

In her frustration, Sue threw the plastic bottle top she was fiddling with at me, hitting me in the face. My knee-jerk reaction was to smack her leg. I felt terrible about hitting her. I had never raised my hand to her before.

Message From The Universe:

> Violence in any form used upon another human being violates the rules of creation and is completely unacceptable. This physical force destroys a human being's love, a human being's confidence, and a human being's self-worth. Whether through words or through actions, violence will never solve a problem since it only creates pain and hurt for the perpetrator and the recipient.

For the next few days, I continuously asked myself why I had smacked Sue's leg and why my response was violent. What I did not know was that deep down inside of me, the wheels of my subconscious were starting to rotate, creating a murky soup of memories loaded with hurt, sadness, and fear. Memories from a time long past were beginning to bubble up into my conscious mind. The stench of the memories made me want to vomit. I began to feel physically sick.

Of course, I did what most people do in moments like these—I pushed the memories right back down into my subconscious mind and pretended they did not exist.

The next day, Sue apologized for throwing the lid at me and said she did not mean to hurt me. I accepted her apology. She is a sweet child with a beautiful heart. I also offered her my sincere apology for hitting her. I said an adult should never strike a child.

Like Sue's actions, which were childish and age-appropriate, you could say my response was spontaneous and unintentional. Unfortunately, that would just be a good cover story. The reality was I wanted her to feel some of the pain I was experiencing, so I smacked her leg. Sadly, the pain was from the hurt I had in my heart. This was no soft smack. I actually left a mark on her leg, but it left a bigger mark on my heart, which left a scar I will carry for the rest of my life. The worst part is she will also carry the mark on her heart for the rest of her life.

The incident continued to eat at me. A few days later, my youngest daughter Maggie seemed very frustrated and angry with me. I was feeling underappreciated since I had made her dinner and just finished cleaning up after her. Let me tell you, a ten-year-old girl can be very messy. I asked her why she was so angry, and I accused her of being spoiled.

Maggie told me she had heard what I had said to her mom about her behavior. Specifically, I had said, "Maggie needs to get her head examined since she does not appreciate anything." At ten, she did not understand my sarcasm and was very offended. Rightfully so!

Maggie asked me how I would feel if I overheard my parents secretly talking about taking me to a psychiatrist. Well, I would like to tell you I responded calmly and explained I was just being sarcastic, but that would be a lie. Instead, I flew off the handle. At the top of my lungs, I shouted, "My parents? You want to talk about my parents? Well, I will have you know that in my home, when I was a child, I would have gotten my butt kicked if I acted like you."

Suddenly, the entire room went silent—not the peaceful silence following a successful intervention, nor the silence you experience after accomplishing some big task, but the silence that radiates sadness.

Maggie said, "Dad, I am so sorry. I did not know you were beaten when you were a child."

The sad thing was, until that moment, I had forgotten I was physically beaten and verbally abused by my parents as a child.

I walked over to Maggie and apologized for raising my voice to her. I told her that her question had brought me back to my childhood. I said they had been sad days that I had locked away in my subconscious, but her comments had brought them flooding back into my conscious mind.

Maggie gave me a big hug and went off to play as children often do.

As for me, I felt sick to my stomach and had to sit down. I felt the room spinning and was about to vomit. This experience had brought me back to a time long ago and a place far away. The place was my childhood home.

Let's get in a time machine and head back to the 1970s. I got my first beating from my parents when I was five. My mother told me we were going to go to the store to get some necessities. I did not want to go. I wanted to stay home and play with my toys. I was too young to stay home alone. She said I had to go with her, so I started crying and complaining. We went to a huge department store that carried both hardware supplies and common commercial products. There was also a toy section.

I immediately asked my mother if I could go to the toy section. She said I could. In the toy section, I saw a little motorcycle I liked and wanted. I grabbed the toy motorcycle and ran over to my mother to show it to her.

She looked at it and then asked me to return it to the toy section. I told her I wanted the motorcycle. She said no. Up to this point, every time I went to the store with my mom, she would buy me a toy so I didn't become unruly. On this particular day, my mother decided to put an end to the toy extortion. She told me she would not buy me the toy. So, I did what I always did to get what I wanted. I threw a fit and started crying.

This time, however, things were different. My mother took the motorcycle out of my hand and smacked my behind. I wish I could say that was the end of it, but it was not. It was just the beginning of a long and painful road that left me physically bruised and emotionally scarred for many years.

My mother handed me the toy and said, "Put it away." I was confused and angry about what had just happened. I was confused as to why my mother would not buy the toy for me, and I was angry that she had hit me. On my way to put the toy back, I snuck into the men's bathroom, ripped open the box, and put the toy motorcycle down my pants. Yes, it was one of the stupid things kids do.

When I came out of the bathroom, I found a security officer waiting for me. This store had an advance security system with cameras. The security officer grabbed me by the hand and asked, "What do you have down your pants?" When I pulled the toy motorcycle out and handed it to the security officer, he said, "You're under arrest for shoplifting," and dragged me to the security office on the second floor of the store, which sat high above the shopping aisles.

I can still hear the security officer calling my mother's name over the store's sound system. He handcuffed me to a chair and told me he was going to call the police to take me to jail. I was scared out of my mind. I cried hysterically. Nothing like this had ever happened to me before. What I wanted was comfort and understanding from my mother, but what I got was a lesson I carried for the rest of my life.

Let me paint you a picture of how this all looked to me. As I was sitting in the security office, I saw my mother heading down the aisle toward the security office, and she did not look very happy. Then, all of a sudden, both my mother and the security officer stormed into the room. I looked at my mother and said, "Mommy, help me!" She stared angrily at me and said, "What have you done?" She told me the police were on their way. I remember asking myself, *Why is she being like this with me?*

My mother continued yelling at me about what I had done and saying I should go to jail. I pleaded with the security officer to let me go, telling him I would never steal anything ever again if he just let me go this one time. To this day, I can't tell you if the security officer just wanted to scare me straight or if he just felt so bad for me that he let me go. Either way, I walked out of the store with my mother and went to the car.

What happened next was so painful I have never repeated the story before today. Although I apologized all the way home, my mother was furious with me and continuously told me how I was just "no damn good!" When we got home, my mother sent me straight to my room. Still shaking from the experience, I went into my room and laid down. Minutes later, my mother came into the room with a long, thick, black belt. I remember lying there looking at her face as she hit me as hard as she could with the belt.

After the whipping, my mother got on the phone to my father, who was at work in the middle of his work shift. In Las Vegas, paging someone over the casino's central inter-communication system while they were working was a big no-no. My father most likely was serving the guests when he had to leave to take the call. During the call, I could hear my mother demand that my father come home immediately to correct his delinquent child.

I can't even describe how furious my father was when he got home and confronted me. First, he came into the room and ripped the blankets off my bed. I was all balled up asleep since I had just experienced the most traumatic day of my young life. My dad grabbed me by the hair and started hitting me as hard as he could. With an open hand, he hit me numerous times in the head and face. When I ripped away from him to protect myself, he pulled off his belt and started lashing me with the buckle side of it.

As the beating continued, my dad swung the buckle at me, I ducked, and the buckle hit me in the eye. The pain was excruciating. My eye immediately began swelling shut, and I yelled from the pain I felt both mentally and physically. All of a sudden, my dad saw what he had done to his five-year-old son and stopped. He walked out of the room.

I stayed in my room all alone and in complete terror that night, just wishing someone would grab me and take me away—far away from all the pain, disappointment, and sadness I had caused my family.

Message From The Universe:

> Although the book of life is different for each person, the one thing guaranteed to all people is suffering. While some suffering is dealt with immediately by the conscious mind and released, other events may take years to be addressed. Whichever road the person takes is fine, so long as they understand it must be dealt with at some point. Upon dealing with the event that caused the suffering, the energy you are using to hold onto the experience and the energy the Universe is using to keep the memories of the event in your mind, heart, and soul are released. These memories then simply start to flow away on the eternal river of forgiveness.

At that moment, I questioned my parents' *Love* for me. On a deeper level, I questioned their respect for the dignity of a child's life. Since I was only five, all this introspective analysis occurred deep inside at the subconscious level—my conscious mind just wanted to play and have fun. Because I could not truly understand what happened at such a young age, and I could not comprehend my parents' actions, the event and all of its unresolved emotions were locked away in the treasure box of my subconscious mind.

Let's do a little exercise to help us better understand my childhood experience of being physically beaten and verbally abused by my parents. My experience is similar to experiences of millions of other children who have also been physically beaten and verbally abused during their childhood.

Go find some clay. Any clay will do. Also, putty will work. Now, let's sculpt the figure of a gingerbread person. First, we ball up the clay and then we softly flatten it out so it is smooth and equally distributed on the table. Then, we start outlining the clay gently with our fingers until we see the head, then the shoulders, then the arms, then the torso, then the legs, and finally, the feet.

Next, we carefully separate the body parts from the rest of the clay, removing the excess material. We are very gentle so we do not tear the clay. We move slowly, attempting to keep the figure uniform and proportional. Once it has been created, we leave it alone so all the pieces dry. When the sculpture dries, it is ready to be exhibited to the world and live its own life. Congratulations; let me introduce you to your new clay gingerbread person. This new person is beautiful and exhibits the characteristics of strength, balance, and harmony.

Let's take another piece of clay and again attempt to create a gingerbread person. This time, let's use only our fists and knuckles to create it. We smash the clay well. Everything looks good so far. Then we attempt to create an outline of the gingerbread person by only using our fists and knuckles. At first, we tell ourselves the outline is going to look fine, but then we begin to see the tears and disfigurement in the gingerbread person. To eliminate the tears, we again smash up the clay with our fists to reattach the torn body parts to the outline. We notice our creation is not very pretty, but like life, we have to continue with the exercise.

In looking at our clay figure, we see it is out of proportion and lacks the structural integrity to survive. It has numerous unstable areas, and the clay figure looks very awkward. Hoping for the best, we let it dry, only to realize our gingerbread person is about to fall apart. Now, we make another attempt to fix it by smashing the ugly areas into their proper and correct form. What we immediately realize is the clay structure has been molded into many disjointed pieces.

This is what happens to a person who is physically beaten and verbally abused as a child.

Yes, I never stole another thing. In fact, the thought of stealing another person's property makes me sick, but sadly, I lost something much more important. I lost some respect for my parents. Mutual respect between parent and child is integral to the relationship because it allows the child to learn from the parents' behavior, the parents' actions, and the parents' beliefs. This mutual respect encourages a growing adolescent to determine which beliefs, thoughts, and philosophies they will incorporate into their life as an adult. This concept of mutual respect is fundamentally necessary to raise a courageous, understanding, and thoughtful child who will eventually become a contributing member of society.

Message From The Universe:

> Humans have evolved to the level of understanding right and wrong at a very young age. But we still have to teach our children to identify "wrong" behavior or they may develop destructive attitudes, causing drastic consequences. As a parent, you are molding your child into what they become. The manner of molding a child is intricately important to your child's future success. If you treat your child like an animal, don't be surprised if they grow up to be an animal.

I am not saying I should not have been punished for shoplifting. I think any child who is caught shoplifting needs to understand the concept of respecting another's property. Stealing is a direct indicator that a child needs more parental guidance and more parental intervention. Maybe no one ever explained to the child that items sold at the store need to be bought before they are taken off the premises. Maybe the parents did not specifically say taking someone else's things is wrong. Maybe the child saw their parents steal or change price tags at the store, so the child is confused about what constitutes stealing. Maybe someone told the child it was okay to steal from stores because they can afford it or they charge too much.

Whatever the reason, as parents, we need to identify it. We need to know why the child stole something. Specifically, we should ask ourselves, "Why did my child steal that?" In my scenario, if my parents had talked to me instead of violently punishing me with a belt, they would have known I stole because I was angry for having to go to the store and frustrated because I was not being rewarded for going to the store. One could say I was not feeling *Loved* by my mother, and therefore, I took matters into my own hands—today we call this "acting out." I ripped open the plastic package and took out the toy motorcycle. Knowing what I did was wrong, I hid the motorcycle down my pants.

What does the stealing of the motorcycle tell us about me as a child? First, it tells me I needed some reassurance that I was *Loved.* Second, it tells me to look at the situation from the child's perspective—I went out of my way to accompany Mom to the store when I really wanted to stay at home. Third, it tells me I put my personal gratification over the needs of the household and other's property rights. Fourth, it tells me I knew what I did was wrong, since I hid the toy motorcycle in my pants so no one would see it. Last, it shows I did not understand the consequences of my actions.

So, what would a reasonable and appropriate response look like? My parents' response was to beat the crap out of me and then verbally belittle me. In short, abuse. This irrational and abusive response failed to address any of the issues I was obviously dealing with at both a subconscious and conscious level.

The first thing my mother should have done was to tell me she *Loved* me. This would have eliminated the stigma of the event and created a channel of communication free of fear and judgment. Then, my mother should have asked me why I had stolen the toy motorcycle and explained why it was wrong to steal. Based on this conversation, she could have determined why I had acted out and gauged my propensity for truthfulness. It would have also created a meaningful exchange of ideas and thoughts between us.

Dialogue is very important between a child and a parent. If dialogue is encouraged, the child will typically be open and honest with the parents. This is important in the child's development because it reinforces the idea that parents are there to listen and help—not hurt or condemn. This creates a feeling of *Love* between the parent and the child, which helps establish a foundation for growth.

This open dialogue allows the child to freely discuss their thoughts and ideas. It also allows parents to present their thoughts and ideas to the child without being overbearing. This one step—creating open and uninhibited dialogue with a child—is very important because it encourages the child to think, speak, and listen. It eliminates the one-sidedness of the parent-child relationship and moves it beyond the child being told what to think, how to act, and what to do.

Correct behavior, proper conduct, can be learned through so many avenues. However, physical violence and verbal abuse are not among them. Spanking a child on its bottom may be appropriate in some limited situations, especially before the child is capable of complex reasoning, but violence only begets violence. Your child may behave in front of you to avoid punishment, but that is out of fear, and they are much more likely to use intimidation and violence in their own relationships.

Alternative correctives include making the child stay in their room for a period. You can make the child write a paper on how stealing hurts the victim—or just simply make them write "I won't steal" 100 times. I bet any of these approaches, as well as timeouts, would help the child understand the importance of respecting others' property.

The major problem in the shoplifting scenario was not so much with me—my actions were age-appropriate and offered a learning opportunity that many have experienced. The main problem was my parents' inappropriate reaction. Specifically, the higher concepts of open dialogue and equality were frightening to my mother and father. In their minds, their highest mission was to make everyone in their immediate family "perfect." Since they were superior to me, only their opinions, actions, and thoughts were relevant; since they were the adults, they were the only ones who could lead our family to the coveted land of "Perfection." Therefore, they used an approach that eliminated equality and freedom. In essence, they eliminated unconditional *Love* from our relationship.

Understand that violence will not control another person's behavior for very long. Some may think they can control others through perpetuated violence, but ultimately, the oppressed will rise up—somehow. I rebelled. The more I fought back, the more difficult my parents became. The more I tried to exercise my ability to think freely, the more my parents judged me and criticized me. The more responsible I attempted to be, the more my parents said I was totally irresponsible.

My parents mistakenly believed a non-violent, loving response would have taken away the control they so much coveted and demanded. They had a "my way or the highway" philosophy. It reflected a belief that life is extremely polarized. You're either all good or all bad—there is no in-between.

Message From The Universe:

Only the darkness deals in absolutes because it is void of understanding, patience, or compassion.

For me, it was my parents' way or else. When the physical beatings stopped, because I was too big, too old, and too strong, the beatings became verbal. Verbal and physical abuse were my parents' tools to dominate their children. Unfortunately, it created significant self-doubt in their children, which paved the way to living in fear. In these dynamics, you consistently doubt yourself and rely on others to make all the decisions—someone else is in control of your life.

Message From The Universe:

No one can control the Universe. In its magnanimous glory, its energy is always in control, and its energy is always directed toward the light of love. Those who attempt to control the Universe will always fall short because the energy of the Universe is unlimited.

My mother's father used corporal punishment to control his home and his children. Corporal punishment is the concept of imposing pain on the body as a form of punishment. It is a method users believe will prevent similar behavior in the future. Although corporal punishment has been the go-to punishment for much of our history, its ineffectiveness and, in fact, its dangers have led school systems in thirty-one states to ban it. Studies have shown that corporal punishment can lead to increased aggression, antisocial behavior, physical injury, and mental health problems.

My mother's father demanded perfection on all levels. When that demand was not met, anger motivated his response toward the underachiever. He knew corporal punishment would motivate people to change their behavior or do better. What he did not understand, until days before his death, was how damaging his behavior was to his wife and children.

Message From The Universe:

> Stop the unkindness. Unkindness is used to transfer suffering onto another. People may believe that through their unkind actions, they may release their suffering, without consequence, and their suffering will stop. Sadly, the transfer of suffering is usually from an adult to a child, since children's resistance is typically minimal. It does not eliminate a person's suffering; it only causes more suffering for the unkind person and causes suffering for the recipient of the unkind act. So just simply stop being unkind!

How did I deal with this abusive behavior as a child? I got into sports. I played every sport I could play. I started swimming competitively at an early age. As a child, I also played football, basketball, and soccer. Basically, I tried to get involved in anything that would get me out of my house and away from the arguing and fighting. After playing sports, I would immediately go to bed where, unfortunately, other issues persisted.

Message From The Universe:

Respect cannot be forced by another; it can only be earned. Respect is normally earned through acts of compassion, understanding, and love. These are the basic building blocks of respect.

I was somewhat of a bully in high school. The apple doesn't fall far from the tree, does it? Yes, for a while, I used intimidation and force on others in high school. I started fist-fighting regularly when I went out. Somehow, I thought violence would show my manhood. Looking back, it showed I was an emotionally disturbed youth in need of serious counseling. Although I never fought any of my high school friends, I sure terrorized them. I am truly sad about how I made them feel, and I offer them my sincerest apology for my behavior.

How did this all turn out? Actually, it turned out all right, but it took me a long time to identify the pain I had hidden deep down inside and to understand the rage trapped inside of me. It took many years for my emotional scars to heal.

Message From The Universe:

Time heals all wounds.

Today, fifty-eight countries have outlawed using corporal punishment on children. Unfortunately, the United States of America is not one of those countries. In this beautiful country, beating children to make them "behave" is still condoned in many places, and I have heard people publicly say we need to beat our kids more. These old-school holdouts do not fully understand the damage corporal punishment does to the children of this country and the world. I would guess most of these people were beaten themselves as youths, and they want to justify their parents' behavior. Just because your parents did it, and maybe you did it, does not make it right. In fact, that sort of thinking is an impediment to raising happy, healthy children who grow up to be strong, independent, caring adults.

Children are the future of this country, so their ideas, actions, and beliefs must be protected! Only through their free thinking can the catastrophic issues that threaten to destroy this planet be solved. Free-thinking children grow up to be emotionally stable, non-violent, and compassionate adults.

So, to the parents who use corporal punishment—stop the madness! It is destroying your family and your child. Every beating is remembered, not forgotten like you may believe. Knowing that alone should make you stop your crazy behavior toward your children.

For the children being beaten by their parents, please understand you don't deserve to be beaten. Hang in there! Understand that every action is seen by the Universe, and one day you will be out of this abusive situation; then you can become part of the solution to this unnecessary abuse. Let your satisfaction lie in knowing you will not beat your children, since you know how it feels.

It is through those of us who have been beaten and those who do not believe in corporal punishment that this tragedy will be eliminated from this planet. Once we all stand up and demand *Love* for all beings, the energy of this planet will truly be recognized throughout the Universe! Again, I say the answer is *Love*.

"Change will not come if we wait for some other person or some other time. We are the ones we have been waiting for.
We are the change that we seek."

— President Barack Obama

Suggested listening: *Truth Be Told* by Matthew West

Chapter 4

Love You Too!

"Whatever the question, Love is the answer."

— Dr. Wayne Dyer

I would just like to respond to the opening statement from my previous chapter with the simple statement, "I *Love* you, too." You may wonder how that makes me feel. Well, I can honestly say I feel incredibly different now that I have begun addressing the issues I have stored away deep in my subconscious. I wish I could tell you that once I addressed these particular issues, all my mental anguish disappeared. I wish I could tell you that afterwards, I just skipped through my house happy as a lark. I wish I could tell you everything fell right into place and I lived happily ever after. But that is not what happened.

Message From The Universe:

Love always starts with the individual first loving themselves and then loving others. If a person cannot love themselves, they truly don't understand how to love, and they will have difficulty loving others. It is through our practice of love that all battles are won.

When I started dealing with my repressed feelings, I actually felt overwhelmingly sick and emotionally distraught. Once I opened up to the world about the physical and verbal abuse I experienced as a child, I didn't feel invincible. I felt very sad, but I didn't feel as lonely. For the first time, my ears heard I had been the victim of abuse, my eyes saw I was a victim of abuse, and my mind realized I had been a victim of abuse. Deep down, I began to understand I had been a victim of abuse throughout the majority of my life, which caused a significant change in how I *Loved* and treated others.

Afterwards, I needed to lay down as the feelings and emotions began to overwhelm me. Specifically, the feelings of anger and disgust would not subside, so I just crashed out for the evening. All night long, I tossed and turned, reliving the fights and arguments. See, it's hard to admit you were beaten by your parents. Some societal expectations say revealing this dark and extremely damning information years later is cowardly and the stories can be viewed by some with skepticism. Consequently, admitting to having been abused is extremely difficult.

Even though we all know it still exists, people don't talk about parental abuse, since most people choose not to deal with it. Today, across the world, thousands upon thousands of children experience either physical or verbal abuse from one parent or both. These children end up with black eyes, cuts, scars, scrapes, burns, and bruises on their bodies because their parents cannot control their emotions. It happens across all walks of life, to both rich and poor.

Here is a perfect example. A few years ago, I heard a story about a professional athlete who physically abused his young child. Apparently, this athlete, weighing approximately 220 pounds and standing 6' 1", was arrested and subsequently indicted by a grand jury on charges of reckless or negligent injury to a child (felony). It was alleged the athlete had beat his four-year-old son, which resulted in cuts and bruises all over the boy's body, including the child's bottom and scrotum.

Now, take a second to think of the magnitude and length of the beatings. This was no simple swat or smack. I would venture to guess it was a pretty intense beating. My introspective question is, "What could a four-year-old child do to justify such a severe beating?" Unfortunately, as of 2018, the father had still failed to understand that nothing a four-year-old could do would call for such a beating.

Eventually, this athlete pled no contest to a reduced charge of reckless assault (misdemeanor). For all the lay people, what this means is the father did not deny the allegations, and as such, submitted the facts as alleged in the criminal complaint to the court for determination. Basically, he never fought the allegations of assaulting his child, so he was found guilty.

I know the story all too well—with money, you get the best criminal defense attorney in the area, someone who has a good relationship with the prosecutor's office, and you all agree on a deal. In this case, the deal allowed the professional athlete to return to his sport where he made millions and allowed the prosecutor to move on to the next case.

What about the little boy?

The child carries being severely beaten by his father at age four for the rest of his life. Typically, a young child in this type of a situation goes right back to the same abusive behavior at home. Instead of publicly apologizing to his son, the professional athlete explained in an interview many years later that he continues to use the same type of corporal punishment on his child as his preferred method of punishment. The athlete said his criminal case did not change his opinion of corporal punishment or how he punishes his child.

In the above example, the physical abuse was brought to surface because one parent was in the public spotlight and his child had physical marks. What happens to all those kids whose parents are not superstars or whose marks are not discovered? It becomes a "dirty little secret" that lives inside the child and the family until someday someone explodes. This cyclical pattern of abuse may continue into the child's adult life by way of verbal attacks upon their character, their beliefs, and their ideas by their parents, siblings, or extended family. In such a situation, the abused child, now an adult, may believe they are wrong in the ways they think, they act, and they feel. Sometimes, abuse is introduced into the next generation not by parents but grandparents, aunts, or uncles. In all of the silence, the physical and verbal abuse continues to cycle from generation to generation without being acknowledged or addressed. The physical and verbal abuse imposed upon a child by the parents, and possibly family members, eliminates the child's innocence and convicts the child of being no good without a jury. It is their family's verdict, and that is it.

With this conviction, the child loses confidence in themselves and in their parents. The child begins to have self-doubt and becomes angry inside since they know something is just not right. This feeling undermines a child's self-worth and self-confidence, which the child so desperately needs to move into the world as an adult. Presently, the destructive pattern of parental physical and verbal abuse is being validated by not only the legal system, which has little room for victims' rights and wellbeing, but also by the alleged *Love* in relationships between parent and siblings.

When I got up the next morning after opening my "treasure box of buried troubles," I felt as if 1,000 pounds of pain had been lifted off of me. I was still feeling the effects of the emotional scars left by the abuse, but for some odd reason, I felt like I was young again. I felt light, quick, and witty. I was shocked by how much more energy I had after addressing these issues. During the day, my emotional responses were not as anxious and explosive as they were when I was keeping my dirty little secret. I also felt more at peace with myself, with others, and with my existence. I realized I was beginning to digest what had happened to me.

The process of healing from physical and verbal abuse is not easy since the first step in the climb of fully releasing the pain and hurt is to relive the events. The events are then seen through your conscious mind without distraction. This time, you see the events for what they truly are without anyone else's comments. You see your perception of the events followed by detailed introspective analysis of how the events happened, why they happened, and when they happened. These combined factors allow you to validate your conclusion. Yes, it hurts to relive the events, but it must be done so you may close that chapter of your life.

Next, you examine the parties involved and their intentions. You feel sad that you had to experience the events, but you realize you will be much stronger and wiser for having gone through the tragedy. Once you tear off the bandage covering the events and actually see the cuts and scars with your own eyes, you may think, *How did these injuries manifest themselves in my life?* In the end, you ask yourself how to keep the destructive behavior from creeping back into your life.

In my case, the abuse started with the irrational thought that children are perfect and, therefore, they should act perfectly. This thought is absolutely crazy, considering that a child is typically pretty sheltered and does not venture far from home until they reach their teens. In the child's sheltered environment, the factors are controlled and, therefore, their possible outcomes are limited. Their reasoning skills are limited based on the principles of brain development and the limited experience they have on the planet. They are trying to figure out themselves and life. Of course, they are going to make mistakes.

The child makes a mistake; you fly off the handle and hit them. My question is: How did you help your child? It is obvious your child made a mistake. It is also obvious you punished the child for making the mistake. Is anyone even taking a second to consider why the child made the mistake? Is anyone considering the child's future? By abusing the child, the abuser intensifies the problem since they become an additional problem in the experience and eliminate themselves from any possible constructive solution.

The child is forced to deal with their own bad decision and also your bad decision—using violence to fix the problem is not a good decision, despite what many old-school disciplinarians might think. That is a lot for a child's developing mind to handle. It makes the child grow up way too fast, and it may cause the child to lose themselves. In all that twisted growth, a child may surrender their childhood, but they will never forget why.

Message From The Universe:

Only great love defeats great hate.

I have to ask myself, "How can an individual who cares so much for their children hurt them so badly?" As I was told many times when I was young, I was being punished so I could become a better and stronger person. Since my parents always demanded perfection, I could not be *Loved* until I was perfect. Yet I was making mistake after mistake and getting my butt kicked for it. Therefore, I was always questioning *Love*, and as I got older, I even questioned the existence of *Love*.

The problem with this type of parenting is that abusing a child leaves not only physical and mental pain but also causes significant emotional pain. This emotional pain is further intensified by parents' comments and actions toward the child during and after the abuse. What this drama tells the child, without using words, is that they must change to be *Loved*. It subliminally yells at the child, "You are not *Loved* because you are no good."

How does the child respond? The child crumbles physically; the child crumbles emotionally; the child crumbles mentally. The physical and verbal abuse can become so overwhelming that some children refuse to communicate with their families and remain silent for extended periods. We have all heard of the clinical cases where children refuse to speak after a traumatic event. Well, a grown man beating a child senseless is pretty traumatic. This abusive event happens millions of times every day around the world to both boys and girls, and we are not doing nearly enough to stop it. Well, I am standing up and saying something right now. Join me!

I remember one day I was playing with my best friend at my house when my father got angry because we were making too much noise. He asked us to keep it down. Well, you know kids—we only got louder. All of a sudden, my dad flew out of his bedroom and punched me square in the chest. My friend was startled. While I was hunched over crying, my friend wanted to go play outside. While we were playing outside, my friend asked, "Did it hurt when he hit you?" I said, "I have a special cream I put on all over my body that stops the blows from hurting me." Well, that special cream was "denial," and the sadness about those traumatic events never wore off.

Message From The Universe:

> Children are thinking machines. They are unique in that they are more observant than adults. Children listen for many years before speaking. In doing all that listening, children develop the ability to hear the message sent through a person's acts and through a person's heart.

What happens to a child when they are physically and verbally abused by their parents? The child is totally defeated and fatigued by the event. They do not comprehend the actions and see no way to fix the problem. The child does not know what to do, say, feel, or think. The child looks inward and mistakenly believes they may be no good. They struggle with decisions and allow themselves to be defined by violence. Yes, they become violent and aggressive with other children since it is all they know.

At this early stage, the child is unable to mount a physical self-defense and would be unlikely to counter-attack because they *Love* their parents and so deeply want and need them to survive. Since the child unconditionally *Loves* the parents, they accept the beatings, and then blame themselves for causing such a traumatic event in the first place. The child almost never tries to shift the blame onto the parents where it belongs.

In their sorrow, the child begins to examine their own behavior. When the child can no longer justify the parents' abuse and the pain associated with it, they may simply give up. The child's pain is felt deep inside their heart where they begin to feel less than others and begin to resent adults.

As the physical and verbal abuse continues, the child's self-worth and self-confidence is severely compromised and eventually destroyed. At some point, the child stops caring about self and stops caring about the self in others. The child becomes withdrawn from family and friends. The child exhibits signs of clinical depression and exhibits sudden, uncontrollable emotional outbursts, since depression and stress have taken over their young life.

How does a child deal with the depression and stress caused by parental abuse? As a coping mechanism, the child's higher consciousness takes the event (or events) out of the conscious mind and drives it deep into the subconscious mind. With the memory suppressed, the child continues to grow from other experiences and events. This process is repeated over and over again, thousands of times, until eventually, one day, the child cannot repress any more of these types of events. Simply put, for this child, the memory on the subconscious' hard drive is full, and the abusive events are stored in the conscious mind, to be relived daily.

The recurring memories and nightmares, coupled with the everyday stressors of society, cause extreme anxiety and frustration. At that point, the child, typically a young adult by this time, decides to end the continuous cycle of sad memories. They see themselves as total losers, imperfect and no good. They see no *Love* for themselves and have no *Love* for others.

How does the child end the sad memories and nightmares? Many children turn to drugs and alcohol. Others try suicide as a way of stopping the unwanted memories. Yet others turn to violence. In this approach, the youth may abuse others, essentially saying, "Let's see how you like it."

The results of this cycle of abuse can be seen throughout society in mass shootings, parricide, domestic abuse, rape, and other violent acts. These events are all direct results of children being pushed too far in their childhood. Children who believe in their hearts they are not *Loved* and, therefore, feel excluded from the space of *Love*, in their depression and desperation, turn away from *Love* and focus on the things that have consumed their existence—typically violence and abuse.

Whether it is drowning their pain by taking a shot of whiskey or taking a shot at an innocent bystander, this cycle of hereditary pain moves freely from generation to generation without being acknowledged and addressed. In the silence, violence and abuse become powerful and destructive forces, causing damage to all of us.

Typically, the abused will lose the traits of kindness, compassion, and understanding and become angry, frustrated, and anxious. These characteristics are fueled by impatience, guilt, and judgment. They are the symptoms of fear.

Here is one final story on this issue. It explains how children see violence perpetrated upon them by their parents. When my oldest daughter Sue turned four, my wife Edna and I threw her a big party. We had all the traditional party favorites like a bouncy-bounce, pony rides, and a performer. Sue was having the time of her life. When it came time to cut the cake, we lit all the candles and called her over. As Sue approached the cake, Edna came up behind her and patted her on the bottom, jokingly saying, "You get a spank for each year you are old."

All of a sudden, Sue started crying and darted into the house. When Edna found her, she was sitting on her bed crying. Sue told Edna she was crying because she got a spanking. She had never had one before. Sue told Edna she was upset because Edna spanked her in front of all the guests.

Edna told Sue she was a good child and the swat on her bottom was in fun, not for being bad. She said it was a *Love* pat and explained her intention was not to punish Sue, but to celebrate her birthday. Edna also said she understood Sue's reaction, adding, "No one should hit you—no one."

Sue and Edna came back to the party, we all laughed, and Sue blew out her candles.

Today, Sue is in middle school and doing great! She detests violence of any kind and deplores any type of bullying. In fact, Sue has reported violent behavior and bullying when she has observed it at school. At home, I talk openly about violence and bullying to teach my children the possible cause and effect consequences of this type of unkind behavior.

The sooner we acknowledge the physical damage and emotional scars that beatings and verbal abuse leave on people, the faster we can move toward a nonviolent society in which we all respect the dignity of life. This lesson doesn't cost anything and does not require perfection, but it does require a lot of patience, compassion, and understanding.

Children are taught to accept *Love* by first *Loving* themselves and then by *Loving* others. *Love* is the act of opening the door for someone, the act of smiling at someone, and the act of stopping for someone on the side of the road who needs your help. It is the art of saying, "Thank You," "God Bless You," "I *Love* You," and "I *Love* you, too." In this space, violence and abuse simply vanish and a person's moral compass is set for the land of *Love.* Hope to see you there. What can I say? The answer is *Love.*

"One word frees up all the weight and pain of life; that word is Love."

— Unknown

Suggested listening: *Solsbury Hill* by Peter Gabriel

Chapter 5

Love Others

"Mistakes are always forgivable,
if you have the courage to admit them."

— Bruce Lee

I hear it all the time. The greatest advice for humanity is "be kind to others." I also hear, "Treat your neighbor as your friend." Well, let me tell you, for me that has been one of the most difficult things to do in such a diversified world. *Love* has never been easy for me since when I was young, *Love* was based on so many conditions I needed to meet before being accepted. Since I did not achieve the laundry list of accomplishments my family required most of the time, *Love* was somewhat of a foreign concept to me.

As adults we face similar issues. Many people *Love* you only if you have the right car, the right house, the right job, or the right number of zeros in your bank account balance.

In placing all these conditions on *Love*, *Love* becomes a conditional response. In doing so, we undermine its effectiveness in solving the problems and issues people and nations face. Often, our moral compass shifts to focus on societal success as a prerequisite for *Love* and turns away from *Love* as unconditional.

Message From The Universe:

Love unifies all people through its respect for the dignity of all life regardless of race, age, religion, ethnicity, sexual identity, or condition. As a unifying force, love creates a vibration where we can accept ourselves and others. On this equal playing field, we can all have open dialogue without judgment.

In turn, we use this conditional perspective on *Love* to determine our spouses, friends, and colleagues. Sometimes, basic principles like patience, understanding, compassion, caring, acceptance, and tranquility are replaced by judgment, expectation, impatience, and insincerity. By letting these characteristics hold sway, we shift away from the most basic and fundamental human building block, *Love,* and invite stress, anger, anxiety, and frustration into our lives. We ignore the all-encompassing principle in favor of the four lower-level emotional conditions that have definitely undermined the one principle that glues us together and is the basic building block of our existence. That principle is *Love.*

When we ignore *Love,* we become polarized in our beliefs and get stuck on "I'm right, and you're always wrong." Then one day, we turn around and our spouse, friends, and colleagues are all gone. We are left standing alone; the people who made up our lives don't talk to us anymore. We feel broken as they move on. We feel as if we have lost a part of ourselves; the people who gave us purpose are gone.

We listen to others speak of our friendship in words like "so-called relationship." We are confused and in pain over the *Love* we think we lost. We are left behind, shaking our head, and asking, "Where did my life go so terribly wrong?" We ask, "What about all I did and everything I went through?" For many, this is the beginning of a ride down the destructive path of anger, self-pity, and despair.

In our sadness, we turn to judgment to help us feel better about ourselves and our uncomfortable situation. We judge friends and determine they were really no good. We amplify their negative traits or actions in an attempt to gain support from others and get them on our side. The question really is, "Are there two sides to the story, or is it just one angry person who is unhappy about life?" Regardless, the relationship moves beyond reality and is doomed to suffer and die in the blame-filled fantasy land of judgment and disdain.

Many then counterattack by exposing our negative traits and faults. They bring their private observations to the forefront, making them public so the world can see what they believe. In this new, twisted reality, friends attack from all sides, and we give thanks when they are no longer in our life. After enough mud is slung, we embrace the end using the skewed facts we created and begin to regret the time we spent with them.

In this twisted reality, we forget all the wonderful accomplishments we shared and the happiness we experienced. In attempting to minimize our sadness and lessen the pain, we lose sight of all the good. In losing the appreciation for the experiences you had with your friend, you have also lost the *Love* for your friendship.

Message From The Universe:

> Love comes from the feeling of equality found in any particular experience. Every experience is comprised of a specific cause and a subsequent effect that someday is manifested. Once you see all of the possible outcomes with humbleness and humility for having the experience, you begin to feel the unconditional love found in the totality of the circumstances. This acceptance for all the possible outcomes is where unconditional love resides, and the ego is not welcomed.

Unfortunately, we too often choose to get angry if things don't go exactly our way. When this happens, we make barbaric comments about our friends to hurt their feelings, and we create innuendos intended to destroy their reputations. We intentionally speak lies about our friends with the intent of harming them. It's known that fists, rocks, and swords can hurt a person, but so can the spoken word.

From afar, we celebrate when our now former friends suffer or when they encounter negative life-changing circumstances. You know what I mean when the heavy stuff happens. We have turned our friends into perceived enemies. With all this destructive behavior intent upon undermining another's existence, we must stop for a second and consider, "Why am I acting like this?" After all, a friend may simply have decided to take a different path. Life is a long journey, and our friend's new path may lead right back to us. A relationship is difficult to restart once the bridge between people has been obliterated. If the individual decides to rekindle the friendship, can we say we are waiting for them with open arms? Or are we waiting with a loaded bazooka pointed right at their chest? Put down the bazooka and ask, "Why am I acting like this?"

The answer lies in the illusion created by our *ego* that makes us believe *Love* is lacking, and so, we perceive inequality in the relationship. In response, the ego, damaged by abuse, demands an attack to rectify the perceived imbalance. This attack does not revive the relationship—instead, it pushes the individuals farther apart. It creates scenarios where common friends and close family members sometimes do not speak for decades. It can create an experience like that of my grandfather and his brother.

My maternal grandfather was a hard-working, successful businessman who was obsessed with perfection. He owned several gambling halls and coffee shops and visited them daily to ensure everything was running smoothly. Once, my grandfather was tending to the cash register while his younger brother waited on the patrons. His younger brother asked him to get a guest a glass of water. My grandfather saw this as undermining his authority and considered it incredibly disrespectful. In response, my grandfather never spoke to his little brother again.

Message From The Universe:

Once you let go of the ego, you will know who you truly are. Once you know who you truly are, your responses will be based on love, not on conditions or expectations.

So, who won, Grandpa or his brother? Neither, since neither understood or embraced the concept of equality. The brothers were unable to see past the experience, so neither tried to move past the circumstances and allow healing through dialogue. It is sad knowing the brothers never spoke again and never even said, "Goodbye." Sadly, this outcome happens thousands upon thousands of times in our society daily.

Throughout my life, I have heard people say, "Marriage is not a dictatorship; it is a partnership." Well, that saying should not be exclusively applied to marriages, or civil unions. The idea is important to any successful friendship.

Relationships only survive through mutual growth and acceptance between the individuals forming the friendship. To cultivate this mutual growth and acceptance, the individuals must be on equal footing. Yet, some of us mistakenly believe that relationships are one-sided, that one person must rule and control the other. That is not a friendship; that is a dictatorship. As one can see from history, dictatorships usually don't work for long. They don't work as a form of government, and they don't work in relationships.

Whether growth and acceptance in any particular relationship is slow moving or builds at the speed of light, the reality is relationships need growth and acceptance to survive. What I mean is people must be equally accepting of the other's experiences and all the possible outcomes of those experiences to have a successful *Loving* relationship. Let's try a simple exercise. Find or make a scale with two weighing dishes. You know the ones, like the "Scales of Justice." Now, find some pennies. Take ten pennies and place five of them on each of the two dishes. You have ten pennies equally divided between two dishes. You will see that the weight is equal and, therefore, the scale is perfectly balanced.

Now, close your eyes and envision how this scale exercise can be applied to your own relationships. With a level playing field, participants can grow individually and together. Then the relationship is free to move forward at the rate of growth each of the participants desires.

Imagine that each of those pennies represents a particular positive characteristic necessary for the relationship to thrive. Each penny represents a particular trait such as respect, trust, compassion, patience, and understanding. Although the pennies make the relationship somewhat weighty, the equal balance between each side creates a light feeling for the people in the relationship.

When a relationship begins, the scales are balanced, and each person feels inspired and satisfied with the relationship's growth. There is no "heaviness," and both sides feel happy. They feel confident in themselves and confident in the other person. Suddenly, one person begins to lie and cheat. The other person is rightfully confused about the lying and questions the liar's intentions.

The person being lied to loses respect, trust, and understanding for the liar. The relationship changes and the scales are no longer level but skewed to one side. This typically creates frustration and feelings of being short-changed. Further, the relationship feels heavier to one party since the scale is weighed down on their side. When people feel this extreme change in the balance of the relationship, some simply give up and walk away. Others continue on, but usually the particpants refuse ever to put themselves in a similar situation and never trust the other person again.

This cycle of lying and distrust causes a rift in the relationship, with the people beginning to drift apart. As one person refuses to remain emotionally attached to the relationship, the other says fine and further withdraws. The imbalance in the relationship is so prevalent that the scale crashes to one side.

The nature of the relationship changes. The participants take a good look at the state of the relationship and, recognizing the imbalance, end their relationship. Sometimes, the ending is one-sided; other times, it is by mutual agreement. Either way, ending a friendship sucks, and it hurts like hell. Unfortunately, I have experienced this type of imbalance leading to a rift, then a split too many times with both friends and family.

Message From The Universe:

> Conditional love is a label given to the mistaken belief that people can only be cherished, accepted, and truly appreciated if they achieve certain behaviors, certain accomplishments, or a certain status. It is the first step in creating inequality between people and is a destructive force.

For me, friends were always very special since I had only one younger brother and our four-year age difference prevented us from interacting much during my adolescence. My first childhood friend was a boy named Paul, who was my exact age. He was from Arizona. Our parents met when we were very young, and we immediately developed a close friendship. We always said we would go to the same school one day. We also made a promise that one day we would live next door to each other.

At first, we played together, we laughed together, and when we got in trouble, we took our lumps and cried together. When my family moved to sunny Las Vegas, our families remained close. Some years, they visited us for Christmas; other years, we visited them, but summer was our time to have fun. One year when I was visiting Paul, who remained my best friend, for the summer, we decided to take all the money we had saved up during the school year and buy an album that had just been released.

We got on our bicycles and rode four miles to the record store. When we arrived, we were very excited to buy an album. This was exciting stuff for two ten-year-old boys with only enough money to buy one album. Paul was nice enough to let me pick which one we bought. On that day, we felt like true brothers since we had bought our first cassette tape together. I played that album that summer until the ribbon inside the cassette finally wore out and broke.

After the record store, we went to the arcade and played video games for a few hours. You know, the old-time games with minimal graphics and high scores. Then we rode home for dinner. It was an exciting summer for both of us. We talked for hours about what we were going to be when we got older and whom we would marry. We talked about the cars we were going to own and how much money we were going to make. We thought the world was ours for the taking. We were the center of the Universe. We were ten.

Message From The Universe:

Everything has a beginning, and everything has an end; there are no exceptions to this rule.

As a youth, I was a swimmer, but my best friend Paul was a fabulous baseball player. My father and I frequently went to watch Paul play. One year, he won the Little League baseball title for his age group and ended up with a college scholarship. That's when we started to make plans for college. Unfortunately, at the last minute, I decided to join the Army, so when I graduated from high school, I headed to Fort Knox, Kentucky, for basic training. Paul went straight to college.

Although we did not go to the same elementary school, middle school, or high school, Paul and I remained best friends. But, while life has a way of bringing and keeping people together, it also has a way of tearing them apart.

Message From The Universe:

Sometimes the farther away things seem, the closer they really are.

After successfully finishing basic training, I was discharged from the military because I was color blind. Although the Army knew I was green-gray color deficient when I underwent my physical, that is not an automatic disqualification because a trainee can choose to serve in the Engineering Corp or serve in an administrative capacity. I was shocked because I was in excellent shape, but they explained they use color-coded decals in combat, and if I could not distinguish the correct color, I could accidently fire upon "friendly forces." All I could hear was "Blah, blah, blah," because my mind was on my best friend and how much fun he was having in college.

Paul had just sent me a letter telling me he had moved into a dorm at the University of Nevada-Reno and met a fun group of guys. He said the first college dance, called "The Dance on the Hill," was two weeks away and it was going to be a *toga party*. Wow! I had never been to a toga party, and I liked to dance, so it all sounded great to me. As luck would have it, my release was coming through, and I was heading back home to Nevada.

> Home means Nevada,
> Home means the hills,
> Home means the sage and the pine.
> Out by the Truckee's silvery rills,
> Out where the sun always shines,
> There is the land that I love the best,
> Fairer than all I can see.
> Right in the heart of the golden west
> Home, means Nevada to me.[3]

I joined the Army only to get released for a medical condition, and I ended up going to college with my best friend. Paul and I had a blast at the toga party. I looked like a Roman senator all night long. Paul and I were so happy being together again. We knew it was the continuation of a wonderful relationship. The sky was the limit, and we would never be apart again.

---

3. Official Nevada State Song, "Home Means Nevada" by Mrs. Bertha Raffeto

Our college days were wonderful. Paul wanted to become a doctor, but I had no idea what I wanted to be. We both carried a "full load" in college, which meant twelve to fifteen units (or credits) per semester, and we both held part-time jobs. I boxed on the collegiate team and Paul played baseball for the university. We did a lot of studying, a lot of training, and a lot of playing. There were all the parties, all the dances, and plenty of friends. Those were great times full of fun and friends.

When we graduated, Paul went to medical school while I went to law school. We stayed close during our respective years in graduate school. We called each other weekly and celebrated a couple of spring breaks together. One year during spring break week, we lost our rental car. We had parked the car right in front of a major party where there were no other vehicles. I guess we thought we were blessed with front row parking for that specific event. When the party ended, we realized our vehicle was gone. It had been impounded because we had parked illegally. It cost us two hundred dollars to get it back. Ouch.

We survived the all-night study sessions, the exams, and the partying. Somehow, we both graduated in four years and successfully earned post-graduate degrees. Education played a big part in our lives. After graduation, we both headed back home to Nevada. Paul began building his practice while I started my own. Our childhood dream came true when we bought homes directly across the street from each other. We were young, dumb, and full of fun.

For years, we swam in Paul's pool and played sand volleyball in his backyard. We had football parties with kegs and plenty of booze. As time went by, he married, and then shortly afterward, I married. Paul was my best man at my wedding and I was his. When his daughter was born, I was named her godfather, and when my oldest daughter was born, he was named her godfather.

Sometime thereafter, we started to grow apart. How is our relationship today? We don't speak. As time went by, we just drifted apart. I haven't spoken to my goddaughter since she was five, and Paul has spoken to Sue since she was two. Sadly, we haven't spoken in nearly a decade—there is only silence between us now even though we both live in the same city.

Message From The Universe:

> There is resolution in the silence. Silence is a significant part of reflection. In that reflection we can see the happiness that existed once upon a time. In that space, we can truly appreciate our experiences.

How do I feel? Sad, terrible, twisted, and bent. I truly miss my best friend Paul, and I wish we could talk. I wish I could take back some of the selfish things I did and the disappointment I caused him. I wish I could turn time back and do things differently. Unfortunately, I cannot turn back time, but I can be different toward the people around me now.

I have said this before, but if there was one thing I would change in my life, it would be how unkind I was to others when I was greedily building my practice by being cutthroat and opportunistic. You see, I came from a home and a city where *money talked, and bullshit walked.* If you weren't paying me, then I wasn't listening. If you were in my way, then I would run you over and not look back even to acknowledge your existence.

When I became a "big time" attorney, I was in control. My clients paid me a lot of money to call the shots. Controlling every situation became a significant part of my life. If *we* (anyone for any reason) were going to dinner, I picked the restaurant. If we went to the movies, I picked the movie. If we went on vacation, we went where I wanted to go. It was all about me and no one else.

Eventually, my attitude weighted the scales of our friendship so far to one side that my best friend simply left my life.

At the time, I saw friendships as irrelevant—and getting too close to another could get you hurt. As a high-powered criminal defense attorney, I became even more isolated because I had to keep my clients' secrets. Have you heard of the term "loose lips sink ships"? In Vegas, loose lips get you a shallow grave in the desert. I talked less but had become more controlling. I became a real drag. The more reclusive and controlling I became, the more I hurt Paul. The more he hurt, the more I attacked him for hurting. It really is not surprising he walked away.

Message From The Universe:

> Time stops for no one. The past cannot be changed, but humans have the ability to change the future. As our intentions change so does our future. If we want a desired outcome, we must change our intentions—that will create the desired effect.

We all have the ability to fix such situations, to mend relationships. It starts by silencing our minds and reflecting on the wonderful moments we shared with the individual. Take a second to think back on all the experiences you've had with your best friend. Examine the glow of the moment when each special event happened.

When you see the moments as a blessing and not a burden, your sadness starts to disappear, and the joy of those experiences guides your path home. You continue down the road of life not focusing on the sadness created by the loss, but on the great times you had with your best friend, and you understand that nothing is forever. You laugh about the stupid moments and appreciate the moments of kindness you showed to the person you so much *Loved.* You truly appreciate the moments of *Love* they showed you. Then one day, you may have the courage to call, text, or email your friend to say, "I miss you."

At that moment, you move the relationship from stagnation to infinite potential. The seeds of *Love* are planted in the soil of forgiveness to sprout again for both of you. Whether your relationship begins anew or not, you feel better because you have again created an equal playing field where *Love* can mend the broken heart. Nothing will miraculously bring back the old times, but there is great satisfaction in knowing there may be some good times in the future. Not in drinking, or going dancing, but in anticipating hearing your friend's voice or just simply hearing that something good happened to them. See, expectation suffocates a person while anticipation excites a person. In this excitement, you can keep your ears, mind, and heart open to *Love.*

In this rediscovered happiness, you are free to move in whatever direction you like, and your behavior is not confined to judgment and minimization. Most importantly, you have taken a course to eliminating sadness and chosen to move forward without any illusions or delusions. Once the weight of your sadness is gone, you will begin to heal by understanding that the memories you made cannot be erased or changed. You then again experience *Love* for your friend and the experiences you shared. Validate your *Love* for that special friend with a smile, and understand that you will *Love* them forever. ☺

"Friends may come and friends may go, but the memories they have imprinted in our heart, mind, and soul live on forever."

Suggested listening: *Give Me Life* by George Harrison

Chapter 6

Know Love

"You are never in the wrong place. Sometimes you are in the right place looking at things the wrong way."

— Abraham-Hicks

We live in a "dog eat dog world." Life is tough, and the only way to get through this difficult paradigm is to be as tough or tougher. Many of us believe that anyone who doesn't keep up will fall behind and be devoured. You have to be as strong as a rock to survive.

When you are out and about running around, take a second to look at others. The world has become a place where people rarely interact openly. First, people don't talk to strangers. Most of us remember being taught about "stranger danger" at an early age. And with Covid-19, people avoid each other.

People's fear of interaction has become so strong that people avoid eye contact with others, and as such, people do not need to acknowledge another person's existence. Far be it to think we would have to greet or address another person publicly whom we do not know. In this way of thinking, many of us have lost the ability to *Love* one another.

We live in a society where every word spoken and every interaction is dissected and torn apart. It is measured for sincerity and analyzed for content and intention. Our fear is we may give out valuable personal information that may compromise us, may compromise our job, or could compromise our very existence. In fact, this fear is so strong that strangers do not speak while standing inches away from each other in a line. Just like a rock, we sit separated from the world, projecting strength through our silence. We live in a world where many people believe that to help someone else may jeopardize your own life.

Typically, our interactions with others are focused on obtaining valuable information that may help us achieve the coveted prizes of an expensive car, a wonderful job, and a beautiful home. In moving toward this goal, it is human nature to focus our senses only on interactions with others who will help us achieve our desired prizes. Any interaction with others that does not have a visible reward is discouraged by society and avoided by many individuals.

It is commonplace for an individual to publicly display a hard exterior. We have all heard "That person is as strong as a rock." When we hear this comment about ourselves, we generally smile and thank our lucky stars for the strength we display publicly. What a person must understand is that this public display of "hardness" started a long time ago. Throughout history, people have been conditioned by society to be rocks.

The concept of being as "hard as a rock" is seen throughout the ages. One occurrence that has been common to every civilization throughout history is conflict between men. Typically, this occurred when two men, usually kings, did not agree on their territorial boundaries, their mineral rights, or on a particular religious belief. Whether it was 484 BC, when the Babylonians battled the Spartans, or 2003 when the American-led coalition battled Iraq, the conflict between men has not changed. Men will enter a war with one goal in mind: to destroy the enemy at all costs! Specifically, they want to crush their opponent, regardless of the methods used or the consequences experienced by either side. The leaders of a war, or of a crusade, do not want to see anything other than rock-like resolve to achieve victory. They definitely don't want to hear any complaining or crying about the hardships of war. Like a rock, leaders only want to hear silence and only want to see strength. It is a leader's belief that their army must be as strong as a rock to be victorious in war.

Let's take two examples of being rock hard. On December 7, 1941, the Japanese launched a surprise attack upon Pearl Harbor, Oahu, Hawaii. In the attack, the Japanese navy damaged or sunk sixteen American warships. The Japanese killed 2,403 Americans and injured 1,178 civilians. This attack came as the United States of America was trying very hard not to get involved in World War II.

In attacking the United States that fateful morning, the Japanese killed innocent men and woman who were going through the paces of everyday life with family and friends. The Japanese justified their inhumane actions by saying that a "rock hard" strike was needed to weaken America. The pain caused by Japan's surprise attack immediately shifted the vibration of the United States. The next day, on December 8, 1941, the United States Congress declared war on Japan, Germany, and Italy.

Well, how did the war end for Japan? I know many of you know the story, but for the younger generations, I believe it is worth repeating.

On August 6, 1945, an American B-29 bomber dropped the world's first deployed atomic bomb over the Japanese city of Hiroshima. The explosion wiped out 90 percent of the city and immediately killed 80,000 people. Later, tens of thousands more would die of radiation exposure.

Three days after the first atomic bomb was dropped, a second B-29 dropped an atomic bomb on the Japanese city of Nagasaki, instantly killing an estimated 40,000 people. This included kids sleeping quietly in their beds and mothers feeding their children. The response was considered by American leaders to be "rock hard." This inhumane act was glorified by the American military establishment and portrayed by the American government as the only course of action that could be taken in the situation.

The above examples remind me of my first day of kindergarten. Prior to going to school, my father took me aside and said, "If anyone hits you, you hit them right back." Well, my mom dressed me in knee-high plaid shorts, brown dress shoes, a plaid jacket, and a bow tie. Although my mother's intention was for her young son to look good for school, I would have been better off in my underwear with a sign around my neck saying, "Hit me please."

When we went out for recess, the school bully Mike came over and asked me, "Why are you dressed like a sissy?" When I did not respond, he slugged me in the stomach. I remembered my father's instructions, so I punched him back. A fight ensued. The school principal rushed out to the playground to see what all the commotion was about. He grabbed us both and escorted us into his office.

The principal separated us and asked each of us what had happened. We both honestly explained the events as they had occurred. I believed that once the principal learned I had just defended myself, I would be let go. To my surprise, we both got whacked with the infamous "yellow belt"!

Yes, I have the distinct honor of being one of those kids who received a yellow belt swat on the first day of school. I was frustrated with what had happened. I had followed my dad's instructions, yet I had gotten into trouble. My butt was hurting, and I was crying. I just could not understand what had gone wrong. I was angry and very confused. I had acted rock hard, but I had been punished. The principal then sat us down and the Universe spoke through him. He looked at us and said, "You boys better learn right now, two wrongs do not make a right! You were both punished because you were both wrong."

I didn't understand what that meant until I was much older. What I mean by older is I did not understand what that meant until I was fifty years old. Using my superb math skills, that is some forty-five years after being punished for the fight on the playground. In fact, I never understood what it meant until right now!

Message From The Universe:

Anyone who believes there is a hierarchy in wrongness does not understand the Universe. When you're wrong, you're wrong; that is it! It is where the introspective analysis ends. It is not offset because of your past actions or your potential future acts. There are no levels of wrong.

Many of you would argue there is a hierarchy of "wrongness." That is to say, one wrong act is worse than another. This is an illusion. It is your ego talking. It is trying to boost you above others by saying, "Sure, you were not right, but you aren't as bad as them, so were you really wrong?" Now you feel vindicated since your wrong was not really that bad, and the people you hurt either deserved it or weren't really that good. You start to feel better about what you did and care less about the people you hurt. In thinking like this, you disassociate, or separate, yourself from others, and you justify your cruelty and unkindness toward others.

Well, it sure sounds like another way of saying you are becoming like a rock. In our society, many of us act the part of a rock. Yet, sometimes, being a rock isn't necessarily bad. First, let us take a good look at a rock. Go find a rock—any rock will do, whether inside or outside. Now take a good look at it. Observe the rock in its natural state and environment. You will notice that like human beings, no two rocks are exactly alike.

Rocks are essential to the environment since they absorb and release different vibrations into the environment. They sit in your yard, garden, park, or street and exhibit undeniable beauty through their colors, sizes, and shapes. Yet, they sit in a solitary state with no interaction with anything or anyone on the physical level. No exchange of ideas, no hellos or goodbyes, no "God bless you" after sneezing, and definitely no caring for the other rocks in the garden. Could that be you? I know it sure sounds a lot like me.

But don't give up on the rock—it can be transformed through the beauty of *Love.* When an artist takes a rock and washes it, removing the dirt and grime, the rock starts to look different. It is not as dirty and grimy. It looks cleaner. The rock's true colors start shining through. Just this little act of *Love* and attention alone changes its whole appearance. It has a newfound dignity and a certain amount of purity in its existence.

Then the artist takes time to study the rock and begins shifting it from side to side. The *Love* in the artist's heart for creating resonates upon the rock and is reflected by the rock's new state. One could say the rock is further changed as it starts to reverberate the *Love* of the artist.

Then the monumental job of shaping the rock begins. Chipping away areas of unwanted material starts to shape the rock. These difficult acts change the rock, softening and smoothing its exterior. The hardness is shaped and styled. The rock then reverberates time and space. Here is where we begin the process of purposeful design.

Any design is based on the artist's interpretation of the amenability of the rock's surface. Once the creator begins to shape the rock, the rock begins to see, not with its own eyes, but through the eyes of the artist. It begins "to be" and not simply exist.

Many things exist in the Universe, but *to be* is a powerful concept. Some might argue it is the most powerful concept in the Universe. It is frequently overlooked, but *to be* directly arises from *Love* because it is born from the artist's intention to let their light shine through their masterpiece. Creation is a mechanism that can propel a person outside of time and place. It allows a person to feel the true creative essence of the Universe, which is *Love.*

The artist and the rock meld, working together to create a message for humanity. Each artist and rock has a unique perspective and gift for humanity. This beautiful dance of creation is seen in the sculpture of Michelangelo's *David*, in the beautiful rock sculptures of Mount Rushmore, and in so many others. When you look at these creations, wherever they may be, your mind is drawn out of time and place.

Similarly, you are mesmerized by the beauty of the sculpted piece and the creative vibration emanating from it. In viewing it, you lose sight of where you are and where you are going. You become one with your masterpiece because it contains your true essence of pure energy. At that point, there is no separation between you, your creation, and the Universe.

Every day of our lives, as "be-ings" we are creating masterpieces. These masterpieces are created by every individual through interactions with others. Let's go back to the schoolyard when I socked Mike for hitting me. That story was created, but it was not the masterpiece it could have been. The reality is, we both missed out on a great opportunity.

See, Mike and I went to school together for many years after, but we were never really close since our relationship was based on fear. Basically, he avoided me, and I avoided him. We only interacted on rare occasions. Now, some would say, "Well, your actions were effective against a bully, so mission accomplished." But that thought process loses sight of our true mission as brothers, friends, and companions on this big blue marble we call Earth.

Mike and I both had wonderful characteristics and traits. We both came from wonderful families. Unfortunately, from the beginning, our relationship was like rocks in the garden of life with no interaction. Not only did we go to school together through high school, but we have lived in the same community for more than fifty years. He was right next to me all the way, but like two rocks, we never communicated. Later, after many years of hard work in the construction industry, Mike worked for a major labor union as a union representative. His duties included helping the employees obtain better work conditions, pay, and insurance. He helped others through his career.

Similarly, I became a prosecutor. Even though I was an attorney, my job was to protect society from alleged criminals and to bring some form of help to those individuals victimized by others. So, like Mike, I was also helping. Yes, one could argue we both did "okay," but can you imagine what we could have done working together to help others. Based on our initial encounter as rocks, the world missed out on a potentially beautiful masterpiece.

Now, when I say a masterpiece, you may be thinking of a popular painting, song, or sculpture created by a well-known artist. I am talking about something different, but just as great. See, every day, each of us, as the artist of our life, wakes up and starts drawing. We create individual pictures of ourselves, of our lives, and of our society. The colors and paint strokes we use determine the quality and style of our painting. These paintings then reflect our feelings, ideas, and emotions throughout the Earth. They are seen by others and internalized. These paintings then elicit a response from others. Sometimes, these paintings are so powerful they touch millions across the globe. Other times, they just create a flicker that dies out.

I know you may wonder how I know that if Mike and I would had gotten off to a better start, we could have created a beautiful masterpiece. It is simple. Our relationship's foundation would have been based in *Love* and not fear.

See, *Love* allows for growth and expansion. *Love* is about reaching out to help others with no expectations. It is not exclusive; it is inclusive. *Love* is about acceptance and understanding while not judging others for their decisions or flaws. *Love* is about wishing others the best on their journey, while opening the door for them as they leave. Love is not about judging people once they are out of your sight so you feel better about yourself. *Love* is the reflection of the times you had together and appreciating each moment as a gift, whether it was good or bad.

Have you ever seen a hummingbird? What I find incredibly interesting about hummingbirds is how they fly. Hummingbirds can hover. I mean, they can stay suspended in air over a particular object for an extended period. While observing an object, the hummingbird can look at it from many different sides and angles. In flight, most birds briefly fly over an object on the way to a desired spot. While hovering, the hummingbird can stay focused on the object for a significant period. We also have the capacity of seeing the object from all sides and not just briefly from one side for a short time.

In hovering over an object, you focus more deeply and more clearly since your complete focus is on the object. Your focus is not so much on where you are going as where you are. Hovering and flying are two completely different actions, which produce two completely different perspectives. Each perspective has a different and unique analysis.

Message From The Universe:

Perspective is everything. It is the embodiment of reflection.

The first thing we must do when reflecting upon an event or circumstance is determine where we are looking from and then determine what we are looking at. Usually, where we are looking from is determined by our physical, mental, and economic condition. If things are not going well, chances are our perception of reality is pretty gray or even dark. We would be experiencing life through dark glasses—the type of glasses that keep out the sun and prevent us from seeing reality clearly.

Often, when viewing life through these dark glasses, everything is sad and frustrating. Nothing ever goes right, and nothing is ever acceptable. So, when something happens, we choose to fly over the situation rather than reflect on it. The situation may actually be positive and could help us grow, but because of the dark glasses, we cannot see the truth of what is happening or has happened. Based on this perspective, we become angry with ourselves and others. We attack the situation, the individual, and/or the circumstances to make ourselves feel better. It can eat us up inside and lead to our destruction.

What if we viewed the circumstances from a better perspective? It's very simple to do. Let's just take off those dark glasses and try some clear lenses that have no prejudice about the events or circumstances. Now, let's hover over the situation and look at it from all sides. As we look at what happened, we see *Love* throughout. Through this approach, we can truly turn poison into medicine—there is no better medicine than *Love.*

Right after law school, I joined the district attorney's office. I was twenty-four. I progressed from a novice prosecutor to a competent and caring deputy district attorney. Yes, I put criminals behind bars, but I never prosecuted anyone I thought was innocent. It was really simple for me—either you committed the crime or you didn't. I never catered to the police, and I never prosecuted someone as a favor.

Now, I must tell you that injustice does not happen often in the criminal justice system, but it does happen. It happens on both sides of the equation. After winning a trial, one seasoned chief deputy district attorney told me, "Convicting a guilty man is easy. You're not a real prosecutor until you convict an innocent man." Well, I guess I never became a real prosecutor since I never convicted an innocent person.

My last real case as a prosecutor involved a charge of attempted murder with a deadly weapon and two undercover police officers. According to police reports, two officers were working in an "undercover capacity" when they observed a possible "gang member/drug dealer" in a high narcotics area driving at a high rate of speed.

The police report stated that when the police officers pulled up to the vehicle, the suspect drove off in a suspicious manner. The report also stated that after attempting to stop the vehicle, the vehicle attempted to evade the undercover police officers. Based upon the police officers' belief that this individual was dangerous, the officers drew their weapons after they managed to cut the vehicle off. The police officers then shot eight times into the vehicle because they believed the suspect was about to use his vehicle as a weapon to slam into the police vehicle. Wow, the police officers' response was "rock hard."

Based on these facts, the defendant was charged with attempted murder, which carried a sentence of two to twenty years in prison, followed by an additional two to twenty years for the use of a deadly weapon. So, the defendant was facing four to forty years in prison.

One thing that clearly stood out was how irate the police officers were about the incident. Police officers usually do not meet with the prosecutor prior to a criminal case. These officers came to visit me twice, and they told me they wanted the book thrown at this eighteen-year-old. However, deep in my gut, something did not seem right. How come no drugs, no scales, and no weapons were found in the vehicle? How come this young man had no prior criminal history?

I started to investigate what had occurred. One thing you will come to understand about me, I will not be pushed into doing something I don't want to do, and I always try to get as much information as possible before coming to a conclusion. So, I started by ordering the evidence collected by the officers and the crime scene analyst. Specifically, I wanted to see the gang jacket the officers claimed the kid was wearing that made them suspect the kid was a drug dealer.

There was a jacket, and it did show the young man's colors. It was blue and red with a big "W" on the side representing Western High School. It did not belong to a criminal gang as the police report said. It belonged to a senior at Western High School who was getting ready to graduate and go to college. That is when I began to question the integrity of the investigation.

Next, I ordered up the crime scene report. The report indicated that a collision had occurred between the kid's and the officers' vehicles. The report also indicated that the collision occurred when the undercover vehicle cut off the defendant's vehicle, which was heading onto the freeway. The inspection of the travel lanes driven by the vehicles did not show any signs of racing or evading. The forensic analysis of the vehicles indicated a slight indentation in the passenger door of the undercover vehicle. The estimated speed on impact was two to five miles per hour.

I then contacted the crime scene analyst who performed the ballistic analysis at the scene. He confirmed that the undercover police officers fired eight rounds into the defendant's vehicle, and the defendant did not fire any rounds at the officers. He also reported that no weapons were found in the defendant's vehicle.

Message From The Universe:

The truth always finds a way.

I had been totally confused about what had really happened, but the Universe had stepped in to show me. Some people think they can hide the truth and manipulate the facts to their advantage. But this is not how the fundamental laws of the Universe work. When someone is lying, and manipulating the facts, the Universe and all its laws are working against the person or people involved. The more energy they spend trying to cover up the truth, the more energy the Universe uses to reveal the truth. The Universe with its vastness and glory always wins, and the truth is always revealed.

Here is what happened. About two weeks before the preliminary hearing, I received a call from a local attorney regarding the case. Luckily, the attorney, Luke, had previously worked with me as a deputy district attorney. I respected his ability and considered him honest and trustworthy.

During our initial conversation, Luke explained that the defendant was a local kid who was just cruising around in his new car prior to graduation. The kid had been accepted to college and had never been in trouble. He also explained the kid came from a local family that had lived in Las Vegas for many years.

I wanted to get down to what really happened that night, so I suggested an informal interview with the defendant. This is rare in criminal cases since defendants are afforded the right to remain silent under the Fifth Amendment of the United State Constitution. In this case, the Universe made the informal interview happen by bringing the two attorneys, Luke and me, together.

At the interview, the young defendant explained that prior to the encounter with the undercover officers, he had just dropped off his girlfriend with whom he had gone to the movies earlier that evening. On his way home, while stopped at a red light, a vehicle pulled up and the driver began to rev the engine.

Unfortunately, the officers did not know the young man had just received the vintage 1965 Camaro with a racing engine for getting good grades and being accepted to college. When the light turned green, the young man punched the gas and easily sped away at an excessive rate of speed from the undercover vehicle. He then continued toward home.

As he approached the freeway on ramp, the undercover vehicle came out of nowhere and cut him off. Unfortunately, the young man could not stop his vehicle in time, and he bumped the other vehicle's passenger door. As the vehicle was coming toward the undercover police officers, they opened fire in an attempt to protect themselves from the vehicle coming at them. The young man sat in the driver's seat, frozen, as bullets whizzed past his head. He then meticulously followed the commands of the two officers and exited the vehicle with his hands up in the air and without incident.

At this meeting, I also spoke to the defendant's girlfriend. She was seventeen and accompanied by her parents. They verified that immediately prior to the encounter with the undercover officers, the young man had just dropped her off from seeing a movie. The father of the young man also verified that the young man was on his way home because he had an eleven o'clock curfew.

Well, after the meeting, I knew my suspicions were right. This wasn't an attack on the police officers by the young man. On the other hand, the officers had been investigating suspicious behavior and had fired upon the young man in an attempt to protect themselves from the oncoming vehicle. Both parties were equally innocent of any criminal intent. I thought to myself, *What a mess.* I had the careers of two police officers on the line who had faithfully served the community throughout their careers. What do you do?

I dismissed the charges against the young man. I also had the young man release the police officers of any liability for their actions since no one was hurt at the scene. I saved the young man's future, and I also saved the careers of the two veteran police officers. From my perspective, all parties won, and as such, all the parties were equally one with the Universe. In negotiating the case, I remember distinctly feeling equality between all the people involved. As I hover over this criminal matter today, again examining it from every side, I know in my heart I did the right thing!

In response to my actions, the two officers filed a grievance against me with the district attorney's office and asked the assistant district attorney to fire me for "insubordination." This did not occur, but it showed me how right and wrong really works. Further, it showed me that *Love* plays a major factor in determining what is right and what is wrong. See, my *Love* for the young man, for the officers, and for the criminal justice system allowed me to arrive at a place of correct exchange and right action. None of my actions in the case were based on fear, but my actions in this matter were based on my *Love* for others.

When you are out and about today in society, try to apply *Love* in all of the decisions of your day. Try to take into consideration all the possible angles and make your decision from a kind and humble perspective. Just yesterday, I was watching a segment on a sports channel where they were interviewing a participant in the Special Olympics. A young lady had just won a gold medal in the fifty meter freestyle swimming event. As she explained in tears, she had begun her quest eight years prior, at which time she could not swim. She also explained that from then until now, she had endured twenty-six surgeries on each arm. She finished by saying that anything is possible if you set your mind to it! So, set your mind to incorporating *Love* into your life. *Love* is the answer.

Oh, by the way, one week after that case, I left the district attorney's office and began private practice. Some would say I never really was a real prosecutor.

"Loving people live in a loving world.
Hostile people live in a hostile world. Same world."

— Dr. Wayne Dyer

Suggested listening: *For What It's Worth* by Buffalo Springfield

Chapter 7

Love Won

"Change is the law of life. And those who look only to the past or present are certain to miss the future."

— President John F. Kennedy

I remember my last days at the district attorney's office. I walked down to the assistant district attorney and told him I was leaving. He wished me well, and the next day, the district attorney came to thank me for doing a good job for the people of the county. I still had one more criminal case to handle before calling it quits.

I was handling all types of serious cases by that point in my career. I remember looking through the calendar and seeing the case against a young man caught with two pounds of marijuana in the trunk of his car. Believe it or not, when I was working at the district attorney's office that was a big deal. Fortunately for this defendant, I did not believe marijuana was a dangerous drug. I remember thinking to myself that the case was a slam dunk since the defendant admitted that the dope was his and that he sold marijuana for a living. My plan was to put a little pressure on him, then offer him a low-level felony plea, and that would be it. I would have finished all of my cases, and then I would say my final goodbyes.

Even today, I still remember the case being called in court. At the young man's final court appearance, I asked the judge to give me some additional time so I could speak to the defendant, his attorney, and his parents about the case. After getting the consent of his attorney, I called the young man over so we could talk. He was terrified, and his parents were riddled with fear.

I asked him if the two garbage bags of marijuana belonged to him, and he replied, "Yes." I asked him why he needed two pounds of marijuana. He explained that he sold marijuana to make a living. I explained that the life of a drug dealer was a short, miserable existence that always had a sad ending. I also explained the effects that drugs have on a person's life and on the lives of those around them. I then demanded that he stop this destructive behavior.

The young defendant told me he knew what he had done was a big mistake, and if he was given a chance, he would go back to school, get a degree, and stay clear of drugs. His intention, put forth by his words and actions, made me focus on his future.

Message From The Universe:

Intention is very important to our existence as humans. It fuels a person's willpower. When a person's intention and willpower are aligned with their mission, they can move mountains.

I then talked to the defendant's parents and explained that their son was facing one to fifteen years in prison for possession of a controlled substance with the intent to distribute marijuana (felony). The defendant's mother started crying at the severe effects a felony conviction would have on her son. The defendant's father was also very shaken by the seriousness of his son's charges. As I watched, I could sense the destructive power of the "felony" label.

During my time as a deputy district attorney, I had labeled hundreds of people felons. Sadly, I knew a felony drug conviction, or any felony conviction, is usually devastating. It labels the person untrustworthy and pins the proverbial scarlet letter upon their chest. It limits the person's employment opportunities and minimizes their potential to succeed. In one silent stroke of a pen, someone's life is dramatically changed forever.

A person with a felony conviction can't enlist in the military or become a police officer, firefighter, or paramedic. In most instances, people with felony convictions can't become real estate agents, mortgage brokers, lawyers, medical doctors, nurses, dentists, architects, or aviators, or work in a casino. In fact, someone with a felony conviction cannot carry a weapon or run for president.

Being convicted of a federal felony is even worse. In the state system, you can eventually have a felony offense removed from your record. If you have the dishonor of being convicted of a federal felony, you wear that label your whole life. Presently, there is no way to expunge a federal felony conviction, and therefore, no way to get back some of the unalienable rights we as Americans are born with, deserve, and cherish.

One thing a person with a felony conviction can do is manual labor. Although many people choose physically demanding jobs, that is their personal choice, which I respect. To have physical labor imposed upon you for life because you made a mistake is pretty harsh. Doing a job you dislike and being unable to do the job you like because you committed a crime is a tragedy.

For those who choose not to do manual labor, there is always the option of a life of crime or a life on welfare and/or unemployment. Yes, most people branded as felons are supported by tax dollars. These individuals live a significant portion of their lives on unemployment and welfare. I have nothing against governmental assistance, but personally, I would prefer just doing something I liked and being a contributing member of society. I think it is good for a person's psyche and self-worth to be a contributing member of society. So, my dilemma was: What do I do with this kid?

I checked to see if the young man had a criminal history, which he did not. I then called him over and asked how much money he had put away for a rainy day. He said a few hundred bucks. I told him, "Pay the two hundred bucks to the court as a fine, and I will dismiss the charges against you."

He almost did a somersault across the courtroom. His parents were so happy that they could not stop thanking me.

I did inform the young man that the criminal justice system keeps track of every arrest and every defendant. I explained to him that the next time he was arrested for this type of behavior, the prosecutor assigned to the case would throw the book at him.

He took the deal, and the case was over. Yes, I have the pleasure of saying I dismissed my last case as a prosecutor to save a young man's future. Yes, the young defendant received a great deal on his case, but the real winner was society as a whole. Now, this young man could take the high road and go back to school to do something with his life. Even if he did not go back to school, he still had the opportunity to choose a successful career or trade. His newfound energy and motivation could take him as far as he wanted to go. I know some may say, "It's wrong that you gave him a pass" or "You should have thrown the book at him."

The introspective question is: What book would you have thrown at him? The Bible, the Koran, the Talmud, the Toro, the Lotus Sutra, the Bhagavad Gita, the Book of Mormon, or the Code of Hammurabi? In actuality, none of those books put forth the philosophical concept of destroying a young man's future for having two pounds of marijuana in his trunk. To the contrary, these books speak deeply on the importance of respecting the dignity of life, being compassionate, and "doing unto others as you would have them do unto you."

Simply stated, there is no book to throw, only a life to be held hostage and later taken under the umbrella of righteousness and perfection. Most likely, the young man I prosecuted for possession with intent to distribute marijuana (a felony) would have received probation since it was his first arrest. For all of you who do not know, probation in the criminal justice system is adult supervision. Better yet, let's call it "adult babysitting." The cost of supervision for an adult probationer is astronomical, as is the cost of incarceration for an adult criminal offender. Both types of punishment have a high rate of recidivism, which means they often don't work!

Yet, on any given day, throughout the United States, thousands of prosecutors hand out felony convictions like they are handing out candy, knowing the effects they are creating. Afterwards, they joke about how they pinned a felony on the unsuspecting defendant and laugh about it behind closed doors with their superiors. They justify the destruction they cause in another person's life by saying, "The defendant should not have committed the crime" or "Don't do the crime if you can't do time."

While at the district attorney's office, I knew one such prosecutor. She was a career prosecutor who was very well-seasoned. She was great in trial and had developed a reputation for being tough on crime. Throughout, she continuously bragged to everyone in the office about how many felonies she handed out on any particular day. One day, I found myself in her department watching her handle her criminal cases for that particular day. Specifically, I recall her handling the case of a street boy who sold a small amount of drugs to an undercover officer. He was an eighteen-year-old male.

This young defendant definitely felt the pressure of the criminal justice system on his shoulders since the deputy public defender, who also had twenty-seven other felony cases on this particular day to handle, had barely spoken to him about the case. All of a sudden, the prosecutor dropped the bomb on the young man. She threatened to have the case transferred over to the United States Department of Justice for federal prosecution if he did not accept her offer to negotiate the case.

Immediately, both the deputy public defender and the young defendant crumbled and he took the deal. Well, in this particular case, the pressure worked. The problem is, when the young defendant took the deal, he lost a part of his future, and more likely than not, we all lost as his fellow members of society.

Message From The Universe:

> The Universe is one, and you are one with the Universe. Although you may be a member of this planet, you do not have to incorporate the negative emotions of this planet into your life.

A few months later, the defendant was sentenced for the crime. The prosecutor came back from the sentencing giving other deputy district attorneys high-fives and shouting about how "another criminal gets put away." I remember her shouting, "If you commit a crime, you are going to do time!"

I remember thinking to myself, *You just destroyed this teenager's future, and tomorrow there will probably be another young boy on that same corner selling the same drugs to the same people for the same criminal organization.* Yet, this career prosecutor never stepped back for a second to see that the young defendant was not the only problem in this experience.

She did not think for one second about the strain and devastation she was imposing on the defendant's life, the defendant's family, and on the whole, American society. Basically, she just did not care. Her sole focus was on getting felony convictions. The more felony convictions she brandished upon the general public, the more money she could ask for from the county when her performance evaluation was done.

Message From The Universe:

> The destruction of another person's life through murder or by any other means is a travesty of monumental consequences. To destroy the life of another human being as a means of obtaining a specific purpose is not found in any religious dogma or supported by any rational thought. It is strictly a creation of the ego and fueled by a person's emotions.

The truth is if she had really cared about her community, she would have only sought felony convictions in the most extreme cases. She should have reserved the scarlet letter for those individuals who were truly dangerous to society.

When I started at the Clark County district attorney's office as a deputy district attorney, I was twenty-five. I was young.

I started by prosecuting misdemeanor cases, which are cases with a penalty of six months or less in jail. Typically, the cases resulted in an informal supervision period and a small fine. One type of case that was always very bothersome for me to prosecute was driving under the influence of an intoxicating liquor (misdemeanor), also known as the infamous DUI. I can feel many readers shifting uncomfortably in their seats.

Nevada is very protective of its residents, and it prosecutes DUI offenders aggressively. If you get caught in the State of Nevada operating a motor vehicle with .08 percent or above alcohol in your bloodstream, you're going to jail. Whether you are convicted of the DUI or you get the reduce charge of reckless driving (misdemeanor), you must attend and complete DUI school, you must attend and complete the victim impact panel, you must do forty-eight hours of community service, and you must pay a fine over $1,000. You are typically given six months to complete all of the DUI requirements. The penalties get much more severe the more DUIs you receive within a seven-year period. So, why was it so hard for me to prosecute someone for DUI?

When I was a young deputy district attorney, on the weekends I enjoyed the beautiful Las Vegas night life. I enjoyed the wonderful restaurants with their great cuisine and wonderful drinks. Then, I would head into town with my friends to have a few drinks before I went to the nightclubs. Then, I went drinking and dancing until the early morning hours. You see the common denominator?

See, you can drink in Las Vegas all night long, all week long, and all year long. There is no alcohol curfew, and alcohol is sold every day of the week at any time. Although I was usually not over the legal limit when the evening started, I sure was near the legal limit driving home at 4 a.m. At that time, I only cared about myself and no one else. This selfish behavior could have destroyed my career and possibly destroyed the life of some other innocent individual.

My main focus at that point was not on helping others or helping my community, but solely on not getting caught. I did not think of the damage I could have done to others or how I could hurt myself; I was just totally consumed with having fun. I consider this behavior to be the ultimate act of selfishness on so many levels.

Let me give you a little glimpse of my mentality at that time. I thought if I didn't get caught, then it was not a crime, and therefore, by my limited means of deduction, it was acceptable behavior. It was the belief of "no harm, no foul." I wasn't trying to correct my inappropriate behavior; I was focused on not getting caught. I wasn't trying to make myself a better person; my focus was on living my hypocrisy to the fullest and beating the system.

I think there is something seriously wrong with a deputy district attorney prosecuting someone for DUI and then going out and driving drunk on the weekends. Then going to work on Monday and putting in jail those who were caught. It is like laughing at others and letting them know you think you are better than them. This hypocritical behavior creates a fictitious class that believes it exists in its own world without any consequences for its actions.

Message From The Universe:

> For every action, there is a registered effect, a reaction. You will experience all the effects of every action you create when the variables needed for you to understand the experience are ripe.

When and why did I begin to believe I was better than others? When did I start thinking I was above being accountable for my actions? When did I choose to compromise my self-worth and my existence?

As I explained earlier, I was raised by a perfectionist who expected perfection in every way and at every level. If you didn't get straight A's, you were a failure and no good. If you didn't do everything perfectly at home, you were worthless and no good. If you did not behave as instructed in public, you were disrespectful and rotten. If you didn't eat all your food and finish every single vegetable, you were unholy and spoiled.

On a moment-to-moment basis, I was continuously examining every move I made and every word I said for perfection. Anything short of perfection was no good. Since everything I did and said was imperfect, I had to come up with a strategy that allowed my wretched self to exist in this so-called perfect reality. My existence was, therefore, validated by my behavior as long as it was inconsequential and unseen.

My conclusion was, "If I don't get caught, then it didn't happen." If the inappropriate behavior was not noticed, then by default, my behavior was acceptable, or as it was identified in my world, "I was perfect." Although this brought smiles and applause when I was a child, it almost destroyed my existence later. This is the basic and fundamental definition of a "narcissist."

Message From The Universe:

> Narcissism is the effect of extremely self-centered acts on a person's identity, relationships, and life. It is an illusion created by the mind, fueled by the ego, and played out through selfish acts and intentions of a person who seems to destroy others while exalting the self.

Narcissism does not recognize the fundamental principles of the dignity of life, the dignity of the self, or the dignity of others, since a narcissist only recognizes their own existence. Narcissism is founded upon selfishness and self-centeredness. It is behavior built on "I am better than you" since "I am perfect"; therefore, "I am the only one who counts." With this mindset, a person begins to believe they are invincible and, therefore, they can do whatever they want without consequences. It is an egoistic response that makes you the "King of the Universe."

Even if your behavior is deplorable, it is acceptable to yourself as "king." The longer everyone looks the other way and avoids you, the more isolated you become. In this isolation, typically, more aberrant behavior is exhibited. All of a sudden, the individual hits the wall since the truth always comes out. The person sees themselves in their pain-induced reality. They either blame themselves for their pain or they blame others. The person may continue down this destructive path or hit the brakes and change. If the person chooses not to accept their reality and continues down narcissism's destructive road, they will eventually find themselves completely isolated and lonely.

The more you try to show yourself and others you are perfect, the more the Universe, through all of its magnificent glory, works to help you see your truth. You raise the bar of your existence; well, the Universe then raises the bar a little higher to show you the truth. You raise it even higher, and the Universe goes even higher. This infinite circle of raising the bar continues until something gives. In the end, what breaks is you, in one way or another.

I can tell you from my personal experience that if you continue down this path, your existence just becomes harder and harder. It becomes harder to live in this reality to the point that you become completely isolated in your sadness. Your shoulders become heavier, and it becomes hard to lift your eyes up off the ground. You can't look others in their eyes because you can't handle the reflection. Your existence becomes intolerable because the bar of perfection has been raised too high. In the midst of such living imperfection, you can't stand yourself. Sadly, you are the one raising the bar and causing all the sadness in your life. It seems like no one cares and everyone is out to get you, but the reality is you are the one who does not care for yourself and who could not care less about others.

Message From The Universe:

> Humanity is always struggling for perfection. In this present existence, within this dimension, no person, place, or thing is perfect. That's the rule!

What is my point? No one is perfect. This truth is simple, yet profound. And it is unacceptable to many people. An imperfect world means mistakes are part of the human experience and are necessary for us to grow as individuals. It means if we think we don't make mistakes, then we are living an illusion, or better yet, a delusion. This delusional state causes a panic deep down inside while motivating us to reach the impossible state of perfection.

As you push forward harder and harder, you simply run out of steam or you end up shattered into a million pieces. Either way, the ego is put in check so it can coexist with humanity. Some people become so attached to the delusion that they refuse to let go, so they follow the broken delusion right down the toilet bowl and out of this existence.

In reality, each of us sets the bar for our own existence. The Universe only raises the bar to help us. Once we see our true reality, the Universe steps away and allows us to complete our course, wherever it may take us. In my situation, I ended up assigned to the driving under the influence vehicular homicide unit shortly after my first year as a prosecutor. It gave me a firsthand look at what could happen if I did not stop my irrational behavior.

My first DUI death case was extremely sad. A motorcyclist, approximately thirty-two-years-old, took his fiancée on a ride to discuss their wedding plans. It was a beautiful motorcycle, gleaming with chrome. He was the driver, and she was on the back of the motorcycle, holding on tight. After a short ride, they stopped at a bar and discussed wedding arrangements.

After a few beers and a few shots, the couple got back on the motorcycle and headed home. On their way, the man lost control of the motorcycle. His fiancée was thrown off the back into oncoming traffic and was struck multiple times by numerous vehicles heading in the opposite direction. She died at the scene. While she was dying, the man was being arrested for DUI death (felony). I was the lucky prosecutor assigned to the case.

The vehicular homicide detectives came into my office to discuss the case with me prior to the driver's initial court appearance. I was angry after seeing the victim's mangled body in the accident photographs. She was a young woman waiting for her special day when her life ended tragically and suddenly. Further, I was furious when the detectives told me the driver was "stinking drunk" when the accident happened.

At the arraignment, the first court appearance where the defendant is informed of the charges, I argued vigorously against the defendant's release. I argued it was a serious crime involving a fatality and requested bail be set high. After setting a $1,000,000 bail, a preliminary hearing was scheduled in short course since the defendant could not afford the bail and had to wait in jail.

For those not very familiar with the criminal justice system, a preliminary hearing is where the state has to establish probable cause before proceeding to trial. The state must show that the defendant could have committed the crime. In my anger and vengeance, I made no offer prior to the preliminary hearing to negotiate the case. I was hell-bent on making this defendant pay for his wrongdoing.

While preparing for the preliminary hearing, I spoke to the deceased's mother and father. They came to my office with a ton of pictures of their beautiful daughter. As they began to speak of their daughter, they said they loved her dearly and they loved their future son-in-law as well. They brought pictures of the couple and said they had been together for approximately seven years.

The parents recognized the couple were very much in *Love*, but said they drank a little too much. They told me both the defendant and their daughter were very constructive citizens who worked hard and had no prior criminal history. They said they had warned the couple against driving the motorcycle inebriated.

During the meeting, the victim's parents said something that shocked me. They asked me to be lenient on the defendant because they thought he had suffered significantly from the loss of their daughter, and he would continue to suffer significantly throughout his life as a result of her death. They explained it had been an accident, and even though their daughter's life was taken, it made no sense to destroy the defendant's life.

At that moment, my focus changed from vengeance to *Love.* For a second, I thought of my beautiful wife and how many times we had taken a cruise on my motorcycle after having a few cocktails. I also thought of all the times I had met up with my motorcycle friends to have beers and watch people walk around. I felt great remorse for putting my family, myself, and others in danger. I was playing the part of the hummingbird.

What do I mean? Well, like a hummingbird, I stopped and hovered over the situation to observe it from all angles. I shifted from one side to the other, examining all possible angles. I saw the pain, the suffering, the finality, the danger, the loss, the sadness, and the happiness of the accident. When I say "happiness," I do not mean happiness that the accident happened. I mean the happiness found in acknowledging the wonderful accomplishments of the deceased daughter and knowing she would no longer have to suffer with the frailties of this world. Further, I understood that regardless of my actions, the daughter was gone, and I could not bring her back.

After the meeting with the deceased parents, I extended an offer in which the defendant had to plead guilty to the felony. The offense carried a sentence of two to fifteen years in the Nevada state penitentiary. I also agreed not to argue for any specific period of incarceration at the sentencing. After the defendant had pled guilty, I walked up to him and offered my condolences for his loss. He was shocked, and said, "Thank you."

On a quiet October morning, without any fanfare, the defendant was sentenced. At the sentencing, he explained how much he had cared for his deceased future wife and how the loss had devastated his entire existence. The sadness in the air engulfed the whole courtroom, and everyone had tears in their eyes after the victim's mother spoke. I stood silent during the proceeding since I felt the sadness of the event spoke for itself. Prior to sentencing the defendant, the judge said something I have always remembered:

> Today, no one walks away from this courtroom a winner. The parents of the deceased lost a wonderful daughter, many others lost a wonderful friend, and society as a whole lost a wonderful human being. The parents of the defendant will also suffer in seeing their son go to prison today. The defendant did not leave his home with the intent of killing his fiancée, but he will never see her again. He will suffer with this accident for many years after his incarceration. No matter the sentence I impose, I will not bring the deceased back from the dead. Yet, I am bound by the law to impose a sentence that will encourage others not to operate a motorcycle drunk. I sentence the defendant to twenty-four months in the Nevada Department of Corrections for his reckless behavior causing the death of his beloved.

The judge then stood up and walked out of the courtroom as the defendant was taken away to prison.

I walked back to my little office thinking of the events of this case. I understood the judge's sentence, but I also understood what could happen if I did not stop my crazy behavior.

For me, this experience opened my eyes to the dangers of driving drunk. Whether someone gets caught or not is irrelevant. What is relevant is that driving drunk violates the dignity of other people's lives by putting others at risk. When I got home that evening, I spoke to my family about the case. For the first time, I truly understood that driving drunk was a selfish act with possibly horrific consequences.

I then took responsibility and the appropriate steps and never drove drunk again. Whether it was by staying home, calling a taxi, calling a friend, or having a designated driver, I removed the effects of possible death, injury, and suffering by eliminating the cause—no more drinking and driving. This simple approach can be used to eliminate any unwanted effect. Just stop the cause.

Yet many of us do not heed the warnings and suffer the lifelong effects of driving drunk. For example, in 2018, an estimated 10,511 people were killed in accidents involving a drunk driver. Every day, almost thirty people in the United States die in drunk-driving crashes. That is one death every fifty minutes. We can avoid these needless deaths by showing a little *Love* for others and for ourselves. This *Love* will stop us from driving while intoxicated and stop us from jeopardizing the health and welfare of our neighbors and friends. This *Love* will get us all home safely so we can see our friends and family in the morning. Once again, I must say the answer is *Love.*

> "Just as flowers open up and bear fruit, just as the moon appears and invariably grows full, just as a lamp becomes brighter when oil is added, and just as plants and trees flourish with rain, so will human beings never fail to prosper when they make good causes."
>
> — Nichiren Daishonin

Suggested listening: *Let It Be* by The Beatles

Chapter 8

Perfect Love

"Let my soul smile through my heart and my heart smile through my eyes so that I may scatter rich smiles in sad hearts."

— Paramahansa Yogananda

I would like to ask if you like pie? I suspect you are chuckling because the image of a whole pie, or even just a little slice of pie, brings a big smile to your face. The great thing about pie is there are so many different types. There is apple pie, which I like served with a scoop of vanilla ice cream. There is cherry pie, which I like served warm. There is lemon meringue pie, which I like served with a cup of coffee. But of all the pies I have had the good fortune to taste, my favorite is coconut cream.

After a meal, a nice slice of coconut cream pie brings me to a place of peace and silence. A time and space where there is no talking and no arguing but much silence and satisfaction. A place where I am primarily using my senses of touch and taste, while focusing on what is in front of me and eating it. It's a place in the "now" where I am one with the pie and, therefore, one with the Universe. This integration into the fabric of the Universe gives me a feeling that I have won and conquered all the sadness and despair that has engulfed my life during certain periods. Now, I'm not trying to convince you this integration only occurs when you eat a slice of coconut cream pie; it also occurs with any experience you may *Love.*

So, let's examine the typical pie experience a little more closely. Immediately, when the slice of pie arrives at the table, most of us are drawn into silence. Normally, we have our chosen slice of pie and finish with a sigh of satisfaction. After, we get up and move right into our day. Some of us forget about our beautiful experience with that slice of pie and jump right back onto the hamster wheel we call life. Today, let's take a second to digest our pie experience. Let us take a close look at "The Parable of the Pie." It goes like this:

There once was a lady who had a slice of pie after dinner. Although, the restaurant at which she ate did not have her favorite pie, she chose a slice of apple pie. She chose to have her apple pie warm and served with a scoop of vanilla ice cream. Although she loved to talk, she never said a single solitary word while having her slice of pie. After she finished, she felt a great sense of satisfaction. She left the restaurant feeling satisfied and grateful for having such a wonderful experience. She enjoyed the rest of her day.

Simple? Straightforward? Yes to both, but it is our human nature to make things significantly more complicated than they really are. I wish I could say that most of us only think of dessert, or that slice of pie, after eating all the food served for dinner. Unfortunately, that's usually not the case. Most of us start contemplating dessert during our meal. Others think of dessert before even thinking of what they are having for dinner. I can't tell you how many times I have heard a child say they want ice cream for dessert even though they have not yet eaten their dinner.

Then there are those kids who never order dessert. I was one of those kids. Whether a child orders dessert is not the issue; the real issue is, "Why is a child not ordering dessert?" Some may say, "There is nothing wrong with a child not ordering dessert." Others might say, "Maybe the child can't eat sweets because of medical reasons." Either way, in my situation, something was definitely wrong. One could say there was more going on inside of me than meets the pie.

As a young man, I was not much into sweets. Unlike the lady in the parable, I did not have a sweet tooth. In fact, I have always said, "Dessert for me is another piece of prime rib." Many people who know me have often said there is nothing sweet about me. See, I was raised by parents who always demanded perfection from me and from all those around us. Any behavior seen by my parents as less than perfect was unacceptable and, therefore, had to be changed, altered, or dominated.

Here's an example of the type of perfection demanded by my parents. When I was in elementary school, I always got good grades. I had mostly As, but I also got some Bs. I was not the best student in the class, but I was definitely not the worst. At my school, one particular child was an exceptional student. He was not only smart, but extremely dedicated to his studies. By contrast, I was more interested in sports.

My mother was good friends with this kid's mom, and they would regularly compare our report cards. I dreaded the days we would visit with them after report cards came out. Specifically, I dreaded the comments my mother would make openly about me and my grades. After seeing this other child had received better grades than me, my mother would antagonize me by letting me know how my grades compared to his. Next, she would attack my intelligence openly in front of family and friends. My mother believed she was motivating me, but she was actually causing extreme sadness in my heart and resentment toward her.

Don't get me wrong; my parents are wonderful people who did the best they could for their children. They just believed a parent needed to push, kick, or verbally attack their children to make them perfect. It did not matter how my parents did it, or how they got you there, so long as you became "perfect"; then you were acceptable and good. See, to some people, perfection is the only acceptable life state. Anything less than "perfect" is failure, and failure is completely unacceptable!

There was only one problem with this train of thought; no one is perfect. No experience is perfect. No job is perfect. No car is perfect. No house is perfect. No spouse is perfect. No boyfriend or girlfriend is perfect. No boss is perfect. No child is perfect. Unfortunately, in my parents' eyes, I was really imperfect and flawed.

Message From The Universe:

Perfection exists in the Universe, but it is not as most people define it. The perfection of the Universe exists in the differences found between ourselves and other people, places, and things. Many believe perfection can only exist in one idea or belief system. The perfection of the Universe lies in the actual differences between all the enumerated beliefs, ideas, and systems. It is this randomness in everything, in every occurrence and in everyone, that is the order of the Universe.

To the perfectionist, their perfectionist conduct is acceptable since they are doing it in the best interest of the individual they are imposing their beliefs upon. If the perfectionist says something that hurts your feelings or makes you cry, it is to toughen you up for life and make you like a rock. Then they believe they have accomplished their mission. If they hurt you through their physical acts and punishment, it was to make you a better person. Once again, they believe they have accomplished their mission. What they refuse to acknowledge is the damage they have done to the person's heart, mind, and soul.

Perfectionists are extremely suspect of anyone who considers themselves a separate and unique individual. In most instances, the perfectionist's sole function is to eliminate any expressed or implied individuality not in line with their belief system. You want to be an individual and display your uniqueness? Well, no way! In the eyes of the perfectionist, you are a rogue agent who has to be reshaped, remolded, or destroyed. You are either exactly like the perfectionist or you are no good. Therefore, you are unacceptable as a person, place, or thing.

Do you know what these comments and actions do to a person? They destroy the confidence and *Love* a person has for themselves and others—especially, the *Love* a child has for their parents. It destroys the child's belief that their parents truly care. Although a child might shrug and act as if they don't care, inside the child is devastated. Emotionally, the child begins to harden. The child starts to believe nothing they do is good enough. The child begins to believe they are no good. Even worse, the child may stop *Loving* themselves and then stop *Loving* others.

The self-perpetuating feeling of *Love* that fuels our existence and allows us to grow upward and outward starts to disappear, leaving the space it used to fill full of anger, resentment, and hate. The *Love* in the child's heart, which they are born with, starts to disappear. Later, as an adult, that person may not allow *Love* to penetrate their heart. The heart begins to close, and the person becomes what is known as "closed hearted."

After years of having a closed heart, a person consumed with anger and hatred may develop what is legally called a "malignant heart." In the legal field, this is also known as a "deprived heart." "Deprived of what?" you ask. The answer is deprived of *Love.*

These individuals do not feel they received *Love* from their parents, family, and friends. Somewhere along the line, they lost their *Love*, and since they do not feel *Loved*, they get frustrated with their existence. Sadly, sometimes they make a conscious decision to end their lives. Other times, they choose to make an example of those who hurt them. Typically, before they die, this person will lash out at those whom our society *Loves* and cares about most. They take their anger and hate out on kids.

Frequently, these individuals choose a place where their terror can truly be realized and observed by all of society. They plan a violent event that will be glamorized by the news and hurt others. See, these deprived hearts have lost all respect for life. Life is unimportant to them because they are always struggling to find *Love*, peace, and acceptance. They fail to see the beauty of life and become nothing more than hollow vessels devoid of empathy or compassion.

Life is a painful experience for them that must end at all costs. But before they check out, they feel they must inflict as much pain as possible on humanity. In their desire for power, control, and attention, they turn their focus to the glory brought about by public acts of violence to satisfy their own pain. Immediately after the heinous act, they usually end their own life. They most likely believe they have accomplished their mission. They do not understand that they have become part of the hereditary pain cycle for future generations.

Message From The Universe:

Only great love conquers great hate.

Many of these individuals take their own lives or choose suicide by cop. That leaves us with little understanding of why the senseless killing happened. If we are going to stop this senseless violence, we need to look deep inside the heart of these individuals.

Upon further examination into the lives of those individuals who commit violent acts upon society, we see lives devoid of *Love.* We also see that the person turned away from *Loving* others and started hating and despising others. Once the person is consumed by frustration, anger, and hate, they typically turn their hate loose on others. At that point, anger, hate, and violence begin to dominate their existence. Eventually, they lash out against those they *Love.* They have lost sight of the beauty of humanity, and they have lost sight of the *Love* a person has for existing.

Now, they are on the frontpage of every newspaper around the world. They are front and center on our television sets and computers. For a brief moment, they are known and recognized. Like many people say, "Everyone craves attention." Whether it is by killing or maiming one individual, or by killing dozens of people, it is all a cry for help! How can we help these individuals before they crack? There is only one answer, and that answer is *Love.*

Let's look back again at the parable of the pie. In that story, the woman who ordered the slice of pie first had to have the self-confidence and courage to order dessert. She had to detach herself from societal expectations and her own fears before having dessert. Specifically, she had to detach from the expectation that women should not have dessert if they want to keep their slender girlish figures.

She understood there was more to life than outside beauty and what really counted was to be beautiful inside. She comprehended that while eating that piece of pie, her vibration of *Love* would resonate from deep inside of her, and then this vibration of *Love* would be felt by others. She knew this would then allow *Love* to grow both for her and for those around her.

What exactly happens to that child who lacks the self-confidence and courage to order dessert? You may have already guessed the child refuses to be satisfied since they do not have the confidence nor the courage to be satisfied. They cannot find their place of peace and happiness where they can just be themselves and have fun. They believe they are not worthy of happiness and they choose to remain unsatisfied since that is what they believe they deserve.

This feeling of being unworthy grows with time and becomes a destructive force in the child's life. The child begins to hate having fun and hate others who have fun. In time, like anything else, if cultivated by the right elements like fear and guilt, the hate just continues to grow and manifest itself. One day, this person, fueled by fear, guilt, and anger, formulates a plan for getting even. They walk into the lives of ordinary people and slaughter them; then they kill themselves. All too often, people respond to the senseless killing by saying, "Well, at least the killer is gone now." But the reality is we all have lost, and we have few clues as to how to stop others from following the same path.

See, that killer was our child, our family, our neighbor, and our friend. Throughout their lives, they were shouting for help, but we chose not to listen. We turned our backs on them when all they wanted was to be considered viable and equal. All they wanted was to be *Loved.*

The quieter or more withdrawn they became, the more we called them "odd." The more they expressed their uniqueness, the more we called them "weirdos." The more they wanted to be part of the group, the more we pushed them into isolation. We left them alone in a world full of despair and sadness, with no one to interact with, all the while believing they could fix themselves. That's like believing if your car breaks down and you leave it on the side of the road, when you return the next day, it will have fixed itself. Sure, miracles do happen, but just as your car will never fix itself, the broken soul and spirit of a person will never be fixed without help from others. But maybe they are not the only broken ones. Maybe, we are just as broken in our lack of action and in our false beliefs.

Message From The Universe:

> Compassion is love through reflection. When you step into the shoes of another person, you recognize their existence and acknowledge their circumstances. You understand their pain and thereby reflect their pain onto yourself. This creates an understanding of the experiences of another. It creates mutual respect for the human condition in each individual.

This is all predicated on that one big lie that people fall prey to. That big lie is "perfection." Since they were not "perfect like us," there was no *Love* for them. There was no patience and no understanding for them. All along, we judged them and eventually imprisoned them in one form or another.

As a former prosecutor who sent many people away, I can tell you prison is not a solution. Prison is and will always be an additional problem. Prison serves only one purpose: to instill fear, guilt, and shame onto criminals and onto those who are imprisoned. It makes you hate yourself, and with time, makes you hate others. Prison typically does this by eliminating *Love* from the lives of prisoners. Which is, of course, only a viable solution in very limited circumstances.

What can you and I do? Speak words of comfort and positivity to our children and other people we know or simply encounter. Treat others kindly so they feel *Love.* Respect others' individuality and cherish them for their uniqueness. Just as there are many different types of pie, there are many different types of people. Each brings a different taste and experience into our lives. In the pie parable, the woman's favorite pie was not available, so she chose another slice of pie that she thought she could possibly enjoy. Knowing that you can *Love* and knowing that you can be *Loved* is what it takes to experience *Love.*

Today, take a moment to show others that they are *Loved* and appreciated. Do not compare individuals, as each individual is fundamentally different, and each of us has very different characteristics. Just like our little quirks, we all have different likes and dislikes. That is what makes the human experience so wonderful. Can you imagine how boring our planet would be if everyone had the same physical appearance, if we all dressed alike, if we all drove the same car, if we all listened to the same music, and if we all had the same job?

Let's assume for the moment that you have the self-confidence and courage to order the slice of pie. The next obvious question is: Will you eat it? Herein lies the challenge. So, the slice of pie arrives at the table. Some of us would just dive right in and throw caution to the wind. Dessert has arrived—yum, yum, let's eat! Some of us would send the slice of pie back immediately since it doesn't meet our expectations of what a pie is and what a pie should be.

Have you ever met someone who continually sends their food back when they go out to eat at a restaurant? Have you known people who always complain that whatever they ordered is either undercooked or overcooked? Do you know someone who is always complaining that the ingredients used for their order do not meet their stringent standards? Most likely, the person is a perfectionist.

The truth is the person is crying out for help. They may be living the big lie. What does that mean? It is the lie of a person who cannot be truly satisfied or happy with anything other than perfection. When the food arrives, it is never good enough and must be redone to satisfy their taste. It is too much for that person to believe in others and in their ability to make a satisfying plate of food. Unfortunately, at some point, they lost their faith in others.

Perfectionists continuously send their food back and miss out on the enjoyable experience of a nice dinner, a nice dessert, or a nice time. They leave the restaurant feeling unsatisfied and frustrated. They are so caught up in their own beliefs and demands of perfection that they do not notice, or even care about, the anxiety and pain they are causing in others. When the dinner is over, they don't understand why there was such a feeling of animosity and dissatisfaction at the table.

Deep down, the negative outcome is materialized through the use of the unobtainable state of perfection. It is a vicious circle full of sadness, fear, and guilt. The perfectionist rationalizes their behavior by believing others are imperfect and to help those imperfect people—and to save humanity—they must maintain their high level of perfection. They do not understand that their unrealistic standards are killing them slowly and choking the lifeblood of the relationships they so much covet. Simply stated, their beliefs are destroying the humanity in their interactions and destroying any potential future experiences.

Well, let's get back to the slice of pie sitting at the table. Some people will take a moment to examine and smell the pie before they eat it. This act of using your senses to explore the consistency and complexity of an item, or of a particular issue, can be extremely important. In fact, it can leave you very unsatisfied and even sick if you fail to examine the pie and the pie is spoiled. So, we look for the right smell and consistency of things to validate our anticipated reaction. For that, we have to trust ourselves and our instincts.

Quietly, you make an assessment of the issue, or the thing, sitting in front of you. After all, you asked for this slice of pie. If what you ordered is manifested and your senses validate it, then you owe it to yourself to enjoy every last bite of the experience.

All day, we ask for things. I wish I had a new car. I wish I had a new house. I wish I could win the lotto. Yet, when we receive the items we requested, we do not enjoy them. We believe we are unworthy of the wonderful experience. We get so caught up in our own inadequacies, fears, and dislikes that we don't understand what is happening. We cannot see beyond the fear to enjoy the experience.

Message From The Universe:

> Your birth into this existence makes you worthy to receive and enjoy all the wonderful gifts bestowed upon you without guilt or regret. You earned what you received—deserve has nothing to do with it.

Here is a perfect example. In 2004, after settling a big personal injury case, I was looking for an item to validate my existence as a top-notch attorney. I decided I wanted a new car that was sexy, powerful, fast, and showed I was successful. My wife Edna and I went out looking for vehicles and fell in love with an expensive top-of-the line sports car that cost a lot of money. After buying the car, I brought the vehicle home and showed it off to everyone. Initially, the car gave me a sense of confidence, but later, it caused me to question my reasons for buying it.

I must confess I never really enjoyed the sports car, even though it was one of the best vehicles I ever drove. I could never come to terms with the price I had paid. I questioned daily whether I deserved such a beautiful car. So, I continuously second-guessed the purchase and tainted the experience from the beginning. What was wrong from the inception was not my beautiful car, but my reason for buying it. Deep down, I knew I bought it to show everyone the type of vehicle a perfect lawyer drives.

There was only one problem—there are no perfect lawyers. So, I knew I could not achieve my desired goal, and therefore, I continuously felt unsatisfied with my extravagant purchase. Instead of saying to myself, "Let me enjoy this wonderful experience I have earned through my hard work and perseverance," I chose to fight the totality of the experience. Every time I drove the vehicle, I disliked it. I justified my dissatisfaction by saying it was too expensive to maintain. I would complain about the gas mileage, the maintenance expenses, and even the normal wear and tear.

When I drove this luxurious sports car, I tried not to drive it too fast so it wouldn't get any scrapes or dings. I drove it infrequently because I didn't want to put too many miles on it. I needed to keep the vehicle as close as possible to its original, perfect state. Believe it or not, I drove the vehicle less than Edna. I lent the car to others so I would not have to see it in my driveway. Deep down, I could not stand that this beautiful car did not make me perfect.

The problem was not the beautiful sports car. The problem was I needed validation for my existence. A struggle was going on inside of me where I believed I was not good enough, and therefore, I needed some material object to make me worthy of existing. When I did drive the car, it was unsettling since it made me look inward. When I looked inward, I did not like what I saw—an unbalanced person who lacked equality with others. The simple act of driving my sports car turned into a direct question of my self-worth.

You have to remember that when I was young, my mother continuously told me I was imperfect. So, I began to believe I was not good enough for my mother, not good enough to be her child. I began to believe I was no good in general. So, throughout my life, I continuously strived for this unobtainable level of perfection. Many years later, I sold that car just to get it away from me. After all, I was no good, and anyone who is no good does not deserve to have such a beautiful vehicle.

Today, I regret selling that beautiful sports car; it truly was a phenomenal driving machine. I regret not enjoying the full experience of having such a world-class vehicle. In reality, it was a phenomenal vehicle, and I was very fortunate to have owned such a piece of machinery. Presently, I approach experiences differently. For example, when my children get their report cards, I try to be supportive and reward them for their accomplishments rather than attack them for their less than perfect grades. Please don't get me wrong. Like other parents, I don't like bad grades. The difference is I don't use fear and guilt as motivating forces.

I don't try to make my kids feel less than. I try to reinforce that they are a blessing to me and I would not trade them for anything in the world. I accept their uniqueness and *Love* them for their individualism. I do not criticize their being different or allow them to criticize others for being unique. I reinforce that different is unique, and differences are necessary for our world to thrive whether or not it is appreciated by society or our government.

These positive reinforcements create a feeling of being *Loved.* They create confidence in my children that they are supported by their family and friends. They create an attitude that there is nothing they cannot accomplish. They create a *Love* for themselves and a *Love* for others. Basically, they create appreciation for all of humanity. This self-confidence and self-esteem is displayed in the totality of my children's lives, not in bragging or showing off, but in ordering a piece of pie, eating it, and accepting the experience for what it is.

Message From The Universe:

Don't overthink life. It is what it is, and that is all that it is.

Confidence in the self and esteem for others is what gives people the courage to look in the mirror. Let me tell you, looking in the mirror can be one of the most difficult things a person can do. It is hard to look in a mirror and see something you don't like or accept. It is even harder to look in a mirror and see the things others don't like or accept about you.

A perfect example of the unmoving confidence in the "self" and the unwavering esteem for the sanctity of life can be observed in the relationship between a special-needs child and their parents. Estimates indicate roughly 150,000,000 children worldwide live with a serious disability or a life-threatening illness. Conditions like cancer, leukemia, and Parkinson's disease are life-threatening and debilitating and affect everyone involved.

Just for a second, think of the devastation caused by hearing your child may die. Your sadness is multiplied exponentially by seeing your child in pain and struggling for their life. This is significantly increased by seeing the child's limitations both mentally and physically. Yet, you never hear of these special-needs children taking a human life in protest. Even more rare is the special-needs child taking their own life. Why? The answer is *Love.*

Something rather miraculous occurs in these relationship. First, the parents recognize that time is an issue for their child. In recognizing this, the parents see any negativity or negative energy infused into the relationship as a waste of time. They understand that guilt and fear only make the child's suffering more intense and the child's recovery less likely. So, the parents incorporate joy and happiness into the child's life by stressing *Love* and understanding. They tell the child they understand the pain and agony the child is experiencing. They tell the child often that they *Love* them and explain to the child that they see them as fearless. This instills self-confidence and self-esteem in the child, which then gives the child the courage to continue on even in the midst of much pain and suffering.

While fear and guilt destroy a human being, *Love* and understanding give a person the courage to accept themselves and others. While fear and guilt make an individual want to inflict pain and hurt on others, *Love* cultivates kindness and understanding. It gives the foundation for compassion, which, in turn, gives rise to courage for an individual to fight on regardless of the odds.

All this positive reinforcement is necessary for our survival. It empowers each of us individually, regardless of our differences, to fight on both physically and mentally. It allows us to put our differences aside and proceed with kindness and understanding while fighting the good fight. It allows us to appreciate the sanctity of life while respecting the uniqueness of all individuals. Through this understanding, a person encourages another to live on and discourages a person from hurting themselves or others.

In the end, regardless of the outcome, both the child and the parent have grown by accepting the situation and accepting each other. Later, when asked about their experience with the special child, the parents usually talk of the child's courage and fearlessness. They typically express their appreciation for living through the experience. Similar to the woman who ate the pie, the parents of a sick child quietly live through the experience, and then after the experience, they happily move on with their lives, feeling better for the experience.

Today, let's try something new. Instead of putting someone down for not fitting into societal norms, let's tell those individuals we *Love* them. Let's tell those individuals that even though life may be hard, we will support them. Let's help these unique individuals understand they are truly part of our community and, therefore, responsible for their behavior and how it affects the world. Let's applaud their being different so they may understand and experience *Love.* Through this *Love*, they are going to find peace and will become a piece of our beautiful existence. I am telling you the answer is *Love.*

"So always treat others as you would like them to treat you."

— Jesus Christ

Suggested listening: *Return to Innocence* by Enigma

Chapter 9

Love Roses

"The more knowledge, the more responsibility.
The more love, the more ability."

— Edgar Cayce

What causes a person to do what they do? Some argue our fate is predetermined and all of our decisions have already been made for us. Others argue we have free will, so each decision is made by the person based upon their desires. Either way, by 2009 I was rolling in the dough. I was a full partner at my firm, and I was practicing both criminal law and civil law. I had a beautiful home, numerous cars, a motorcycle, a boat, a wonderful wife, and two beautiful children. It seemed that I had it all. But I was looking for more. I had always been selfish because I didn't trust anyone else to be there for me except me.

One spring morning, as I was walking to court, I asked for something very special. I looked into the clouds and said, "I am so blessed, and I *Love* helping people so much. My life is great, but instead of changing one person's life at a time, I wish I could change millions of people's lives."

As a lawyer, I was able to help all kinds of people. I helped people hurt by others and helped people who hurt others. Although I was able to help so many people as a lawyer, I could only help one person at a time. My help for others happened on a "case by case" basis limited by time and space. On that particular spring morning, the pure energy of my thoughts and the pure energy brought about by the sincerity of my words were heard across the three levels of existence—the past, the present, and the future. At that moment, my life started to change.

Message From The Universe:

> All requests are heard. A request to help others is the intention of love put into action. If made with a sincere heart with no expectation of gain, all the forces in the Universe will align to help achieve the desired result.

I had a difficult upbringing, yet I was pampered in many respects. From a materialistic standpoint, I had all the clothes, all the toys, and all the games I wanted. I also went to the best schools, which provided me with a wonderful education with wonderful teachers to teach and guide me. I never tried to hurt anyone, but I would be lying if I said I did not hurt others, including my family and my friends. Deep in my heart, I tried to be compassionate and giving. On some days, I maintained a sincere respect for the wellbeing of others. Then one day, in my clarity, I heard the question, "Would you die to save another?" Looking back, I know what my answer was then, and I now realize what my answer is today.

Message From The Universe:

> Upon being born, every human being owes a death. Death is a function of life. Both birth and death operate jointly as an experience of life, which motivates humans to grow during their lifetimes. Most people believe death only happens once in their lifetime. Yet, death, like rebirth, is happening constantly throughout a person's existence.

I have died many times during my lifetime. Death comes and visits us all many times. Although many of us believe death only visits once, most of us experience many different types of death during our lives. Whether it is the loss of a friend, the loss of our identity, or the loss of money, it is all related to the finality intrinsically connected to the death of the body.

Many cringe at talk about death, but from a rational perspective, death is liberating and allows for expansion. In death, one starts anew with limitless possibilities and limitless potential outcomes. How can I say that? Let's take a look at someone diagnosed with a terminal disease.

When I was a young man, my godfather found out he had pancreatic cancer. He was a strong man who was formally in the Spanish military and arrived in the United States in the 1960s. In the United States, he became a barber and also worked as a bartender. He worked two jobs for more than forty years until he found out he had cancer. In less than six months, he lost sixty pounds, and toward the end, he could not even look at food because it made him feel like vomiting.

One day, I overheard him talking with his wife, my godmother. He told her he was in excruciating pain. As he was hunched over the windowsill, he told her his time was short. A few weeks later, he was gone. Death had come to take away his pain and liberate him from the confinement of his body.

I remember him waiting for death calmly and graciously. I was so proud of how he handled such a painful situation. He died at home, in his bed, surrounded by those he *Loved.* With his final breath, he said, "I am going home."

We are not going to talk about where we go when we die. I don't really know. What I can tell you is we all die, and I have experienced death many times.

My first death happened when I was a young boy. I had the great opportunity to know my paternal grandfather or *abuelo* (grandpa) in Spanish. He was a quiet man who migrated to the United States around 1974. In Cuba, he worked as a longshoreman, so he was in great shape in his old age. He and I spent many hours playing baseball and riding our bikes around the neighborhood. He was my best friend and my biggest advocate as a child.

In 1978, my *abuelo* found out he had both prostate cancer and pulmonary (lung) cancer. Although the prostate cancer was slow moving, the pulmonary cancer was very aggressive. As time passed, he became more and more feeble. On the afternoon of September 22, 1980, my *abuelo* died at the hospital. Although I had asked to visit the hospital many times, I was never allowed to see him to say goodbye. When he died, I was not allowed to go to his funeral since my parents thought I was too young to experience death. On the day of my *abuelo's* funeral I asked my parents to play a song for him, which I picked out for the occasion. Unfortunately, my parents denied my request and refused to play the song at my grandfather's funeral. On that day, some of my respect for my parents died.

Another death occurred within me toward the end of college. During the summer of my freshman year, I met a nice girl who was also from Las Vegas. Actually, she had gone to school right down the street from my house, and her father was a local attorney. Her father played a very important part in my life and a very important part in me becoming an attorney. He was a kind and patient man who was incredibly intelligent. He had graduated from college with a degree in nuclear engineering and later became a lawyer.

One day I asked him, "Why did you leave the nuclear test site and become a lawyer?" He said his goal was to help others and his previous field was mainly about destruction.[4] This was the first time I had heard about helping others from another living person.

I dated his daughter throughout college, and during my junior year, I decided to ask her to marry me. I worked hard to save money to buy her a one-sixteenth-carat diamond. Besides going to classes, I worked two jobs the whole year to buy that ring. Then I asked her to marry me. She said, "Yes."

I started my senior year energized and excited about my future. Unfortunately, sometime that year, my beautiful bride-to-be became

---

4. Scientist J. Robert Oppenheimer said, "Now I am become death, the destroyer of worlds" immediately following the detonation of the first Atomic Bomb in White Sands, New Mexico, on July, 16, 1945.

fed up with our long-distance relationship. We split up late in my senior year. On the day we said our final goodbye, another part of me died. It was the part of me that believed in relationships.

My next death occurred shortly after I asked the Universe to let me help millions of people. I would like to tell you it was a quick death, but it wasn't. It was long and arduous. It was extremely painful and lasted many years. At the end of 2010, my office manager and legal assistant came into my office and said, "I need to ask you a question." This wasn't just any employee. She was my most faithful employee, and she had been with me for more than ten years. She had stuck with me through thick and thin. She was smart, loyal, trustworthy, understanding, patient, and compassionate. Did I mention she was trustworthy and loyal?

I had a special relationship with this woman and still consider her my true sister. She had helped build the practice, which was productive and very successful. With her help, I typically completed around 100 cases a year. That's a lot of cases for one year. I have always said that an attorney is only as good as their staff. She was a phenomenal employee. She really made me shine both with clients and in the courtroom.

She asked, "Do you really need me here?"

"Of course I need you," I said. I said the office could not function without her. She said she had been offered a job by the department of defense running their legal department. It came with a significant raise. She said they offered great benefits, including great medical and a retirement package.

After discussing the options, I looked at her and said, “It’s going to break my heart to see you leave, but you must take the job.” I knew the job was in her and her family’s best interest. Knowing all this, how could I have kept her?

Shortly after she left, my brother Jed took over as the new office manager. Since Jed did not have any legal experience, we hired a young paralegal who had worked at another local law office to assist us with civil cases. One of the first things Jed did as office manager was to demand that I fire my father, who was the office runner. Although I knew deep down I should not terminate my dad, I fired him and ended up paying dearly for my mistake. Now, with my father gone, the chicken coop was ripe for the taking. What I mean is that no one was around to observe the behavior and actions of my new paralegal.

Message From The Universe:

> Understand that every act, statement, and thought you do or have is recorded by the Universe.

By this point, my father was a very different person from the person I had grown up with. He was patient, understanding, and extremely loyal. He had become very soft spoken and kind. He was always on time and was honest as the day was long.

Even without my father’s presence in the office, I thought things were working well—but looks can be deceiving. One day in July of 2013, I walked out of my home to find the street full of FBI agents.

I was about to get into my car when an agent ran up to me and said, "FBI. I have a federal search warrant." I will never forget Edna being escorted outside by FBI agents with my daughters crying in her arms.

An agent explained I was under investigation for the short sale of my home to a family member. They went through every inch of my home, looking for illegal drugs, illegal weapons, and money obtained from illegal sources. Interestingly enough, while executing the warrant, the agent in charge of the investigation left the keys to his apartment in my home. Edna found the keys on the center of the kitchen island and asked if they were mine. When we realized the keys belonged to the agent, I contacted him to return his keys.

Later that evening, I met the young FBI agent down the street to give him the keys. When he arrived, he said he had just moved to town a few weeks before, and his only case here was my short sale case. He was very apologetic about leaving the keys behind and left right away. What I found interesting was that the FBI had brought an agent all the way from Illinois to investigate me for the short sale of my home. Although no contraband or any other illegal items were found in my home, the FBI considered me "big time."

Yes, I was one of the idiots who sold his home to a family member during the housing collapse of 2009. Although there was no loss to the bank, it is considered a technical violation as it is not an arm's length transaction to a non-familial third party. Yes, I became one of the few people prosecuted for a HUD[5] violation. In May of 2015, on an early spring morning, I pled guilty to making a false statement

---

5. "HUD" acronym for United States Department of Interior, Division of Housing and Urban Development.

on a federal loan application (a felony) and was sentenced to two years' probation. The state bar association suspended my law license for two years. Although I successfully completed probation without any issues, and I never had any other criminal violation in my life, I will wear that felon label for as long as I live.

Losing my license to practice law was one of the hardest things I have ever experienced. You have to understand I was one of those kids who went straight through college earning my bachelor's degree in four years. Then I went directly to law school and finished that in three years. At age twenty-five, I went directly into the field, and by the next year, I was putting people behind bars as a county prosecutor. Losing my license stripped me of the only thing I had ever identified with, which was being an attorney. On that day, my identity as an attorney died.

Let's take a look at the timeline of my life so far. In 2009, I was flying high as a powerful and successful local criminal defense attorney. By 2015, I was a felon and on federal probation with my law license suspended and my law office closed by mandate of the state supreme court. With all these challenges and issues, did I get the message? No! I did not get the message; I was too caught up in the debris of what I interpreted at that time as the destruction of my life.

What happened next? The Universe, in its magnificent glory, continued pushing me to get the message, but I am very hardheaded. While closing down my office in June of 2015, I noticed the new paralegal had spent significant time working on the office database and server. Later, as I went through the office server, which held all of the client files, I noticed numerous files had been deleted. I checked the office database, but it did not reflect any saved files.

In a panic, I reached out to the paralegal to see what had happened and to see if I could locate the hard copies that were kept in storage. I never heard back from my paralegal. When I went to the storage facility, I found eighty-four files missing. These files corresponded to the client files that had been deleted from the database and server.

I felt ill and began to panic. I started to fall apart because I could not believe what I was seeing. Once again, death had entered my life, and I could not believe I was the victim of a crime. On that day, the respect and the belief I had in that particular coworker died.

Message From The Universe:

> Most people view problems as negative experiences that only create suffering and pain. In actuality, your problems are there to liberate you from the things holding you back. You should celebrate your problems because in their truth you will be set free.

Suddenly, out of nowhere, help arrived. An old friend who had retired from the police department called to cheer me up. He had heard I was going through a rough time. After reminding me I was a good person and I had helped hundreds of people, he vowed to help me with this new problem. Although my emotions were spinning out of control, he reassured me we would get to the bottom of this. He told me he already had an idea of what had happened.

The next day, my friend brought a computer forensic specialist to my office to reconstruct my database and server, which had been wiped clean by the paralegal. Next, I hired a certified forensic accountant to reconcile the office accounts. My friend also began to investigate what had happened.

The investigation revealed the paralegal had stolen approximately $800,000. Specifically, she was issuing checks without my knowledge directly to her family and friends from the law firm's trust account. And my friend found out my paralegal was actually a "confidential informant," working for the drug enforcement agency, who had been planted in my office to get information about me and the other attorneys working in that building. Did you just say, "Wow!" It felt as though my soul had been ripped from my body. On that day, you can say some of my respect for and some of my belief in the government of the United States died.

In 2017, the state bar weighed in on my new issue regarding the theft of funds from my trust account by a confidential informant embedded in the firm by a government agency. In my more than twenty years of practicing law, the short sale of my home and the theft were the only two issues I ever had with the state bar. In response to my extensive investigation and our conclusive findings of criminal conduct, the state bar decided to continue its attack on me.

Obviously, the state bar felt my family and I had not suffered enough. Although I had shown them the new paralegal was involved in a sophisticated criminal money scheme with multiple co-conspirators, of which I played no part, at the request of the state bar of Nevada, the Nevada Supreme Court decided to add an additional three years to my suspension.

Further, they said I was solely responsible for the money stolen from my office, and I would have to pay back every cent stolen if I ever wanted to be reinstated. Interestingly enough, the state bar never offered to help repay any of my clients who were victimized by my paralegal and her cohorts. Their only interest was to make an example of me, my family, and my whole situation. It is true some people like to kick you when you're down. I know because I saw it happen to me. On that day, my *Love* for my profession, my colleagues, and the state bar died somewhat.

How did I handle this? I became sad and withdrawn. See, I had tried to be a good son, a good person, a good father, a good lawyer, and a contributing member of society, but regardless, this had happened. I cried out "Why?" Edna and my daughters suffered so much while these people viciously attacked and tried to destroy me. I fell into a great depression and even contemplated suicide. Yet, deep down, something very different was happening.

Message From The Universe:

> Every person has a mission to complete during their life that is directly tied to the further enlightenment of their being. Although each mission is different for each person, this mission is the single most important happening of that person's life. A person's whole existence is in tune with their mission from the day of their birth.

Death, in its magnanimous fashion, had taken so many different things from me. Many of my longtime friends stayed away since appearances were everything, and I had become a criminal in their eyes. Death had also taken my profession and many of my colleagues away after I lost my law license. Death had also taken my identity since I was no longer an attorney. Death had also ended some of my familial relationships because now I was deemed worthless.

As I stood there looking into the mirror of my life, I saw myself for what I truly was. I was a person broken not because of all the death I had experienced, but because I could not find *Love.* My biggest problem was I had no understanding of *Love.* That's when I realized my mission in life was to find *Love* and to help others find *Love.* I had looked in all the wrong places to find unconditional *Love.* Well, it was sitting there right in front of my face all along.

Message From The Universe:

> Love always starts with loving oneself. Once people love themselves, they can love others.

How did I stop this vicious cycle of continual destruction that had manifested itself throughout my life? First, I stopped trying to find happiness in the darkness. Next, I accepted my problems and viewed them as gifts to help me transition. I began to understand the true nature of life.

If I would not have gone through all the trials and tribulations, I would have continued on with my selfish life full of anger, frustration, lies, and despair. Most likely, I would have continued down the road searching for that "pot of gold" at the end of the long, dark night. I can tell you now that it does not exist. I would have continued to take others for granted and continued my unkind behavior.

I would have continued to walk away from my mission instead of attempting to complete it.

In all the frustration and sadness associated with the loss of myself and my mission, I would have created a tragic ending for my life. Luckily for me, the excess baggage—like fake friends, fake family, fake colleagues, fake identities, and fake lives—mostly disappeared, and I could finally see myself and my true mission. I could also begin to contemplate how to complete my mission. What was my mission?

During my reflection upon all the "deaths" my persona has experienced, I found one common thread: *Love.* When I was young, I internalized all the abuse because I *Loved* my parents and did not want to hurt them by telling others about the abuse. What pushed me through college and law school was my *Love* for knowledge and my *Love* for the law. What pushed me as a deputy district attorney was my *Love* for helping individuals victimized by others. What pushed me through my twenty years of private practice was the *Love* I had for helping others who found themselves in horrible situations. What made me reconstruct my office after the destruction brought on by my paralegal was the *Love* I had for my clients. What made me fight so the state bar did not revoke my license was my *Love* for being an attorney.

Message From The Universe:

What you feel in your heart engulfs your thoughts. Your thoughts dictate your actions. Your actions create your reality. Your reality creates what you feel in your heart. This is the circle of life.

As I told you earlier, I understand what my mission is now! My mission is to feel *Love* and help others feel *Love.* My mission is to let people know that by *Loving* your truth, you can turn those painful experiences into a powerful medicine that will not only help you heal but also help you succeed.

Love will help you replace unkindness with kindness.

So how am I going to complete my mission? Part of my mission was writing this book, which contains a message of inspiration and *Love* for all people. Hey, if I can make it with all my setbacks and with all the problems I have experienced, so can you—so can anyone! I see clearly that my focus from this day forward is not so much on being an attorney, but on writing to help others, who, like me, never had an idea of what *Love* is. My focus will be on helping those people who don't understand the power of being kind, understanding, and compassionate toward themselves and others, regardless of the circumstances.

I was able to recognize my mission by accepting my truth. My truth includes every event, every moment, every thought, every action, and every consequence of my life. My truth includes all my successes and failures. It incorporates all the joy, happiness, death, and sorrow. In accepting my truth, I have accepted my mission, and today, I ride the wave of *Love* in trying to bring acceptance, compassion, and understanding into your life.

These three little actions, which are incorporated into the concept of being kind, will drastically change your present reality, and they will also change your feelings, thoughts, and actions. At that moment, you will have begun a new life where those whom you treat kindly will also treat you kindly. In the ebb and flow of this newfound energy, you will begin to take yourself a little less seriously, and you will begin to take your mission a lot more seriously. You will start healing by accepting your truth and the truth of your mission.

So, today, my friend, know that I have felt your pain because I have died many deaths in my lifetime, and like you, I have struggled on. Know that I have been called many derogatory names and ridiculed for being myself by both family and friends whom I cared for dearly and tried to help. I have been abandoned by my profession and my colleagues. I have found myself lost in my pain with the walls falling down around me. In all the agony and despair, know that you can stand up and get back on the road of life to complete your mission. How? You already know the answer—it is *Love.*

"The only way to achieve the impossible is to believe it is possible."

— Charles Kinsleigh

Suggested listening: *The Rose* by Bette Midler

Chapter 10

Love Lite

"The tiny seed knew that in order to grow it needed to be dropped in the dirt, covered in darkness, and struggle to reach the light."

— Sandra King

When I was a child, I was afraid of the dark. Remember, I was a bedwetter, and I was continuously told I was "no good." On any given night, I would sit in my room alone with all that negativity and cry about my life. I could feel the darkness swirling around me, so I always turned on my little night-light.

You see, my little night-light was my lifeline, keeping me safe through the night. Although I was surrounded by darkness, the light emitted from that small bulb was sufficient to dispel all the darkness in my mind trying to consume my life. Every night was a battle between the sadness in my heart and the hope of finding the *Love* I desired and needed as a child. On any given night, my wishes were that I would be a better child, a better son, and a better brother. Throughout my struggle, I never lost the faith my little night-light provided.

Message From The Universe:

> Faith is the belief that a person can and will transcend any obstacle they encounter and the understanding that all roads lead home.

The first time I came across drugs, I was ten years old. My uncle Jack had left his pack of cigarettes unattended, so like many young children would do, I grabbed the pack to smoke some cigarettes. Typically, I would mimic my uncle's behavior because I thought he was the coolest man in the world. When I opened the pack, there was one cigarette that looked different. It was not neatly packaged like the others, and it did not have a yellow filter at the end. It looked more like a football than a normal cigarette, so I snuck off and smoked it. When I finished smoking this special cigarette, I noticed some of my sadness was gone.

After smoking this special cigarette, I felt lightheaded, airy, and very hungry. Everything seemed very funny. Once I came back inside, I asked Uncle Jack if I could have something to eat. He ordered a large pepperoni pizza, which we devoured. I was still hungry, so I asked for some more food. So Uncle Jack made me a peanut-butter-and-jelly sandwich. I devoured the PBJ sandwich and then told Uncle Jack I was still hungry. He started to sense something was not right.

Uncle Jack checked his pack of smokes and then asked, "Hey, little dude, did you smoke any of my cigarettes?" When I said no, he asked me to be honest. Like I said, my uncle was my biggest hero. He was a veteran of the United States Marine Corps, and after he left the military, he became a cement finisher. He was good-looking, strong, and never raised his hand to me. So when he asked, I said, "Yes, sir, I smoked one of your cigarettes."

He opened the pack and asked, "Which one did you smoke?"

I said, "I smoked the weird-looking, fat one."

Uncle Jack laughed, then went into the kitchen and cooked me a huge steak. I devoured it, and then we played board games for the rest of the evening. He kept smiling at me, and said, "Little buddy, you're crazy."

I laughed and eventually fell asleep in his arms.

The next time I smoked marijuana, I was eighteen. I went to a very prestigious private high school in town that had a great football program. In fact, my high school had won the state football title more times than any other high school. In my senior year, our team lost the zone championship game, and I was extremely upset over the loss.

After the game, I was driving home with my girlfriend Paula when she pulled out a marijuana cigarette. She asked, "Do you want to have a smoke?" I said, "I'm sorry, but I don't do drugs." She said, "It will take your pain away." So I smoked with her that evening. It made me feel better inside since I was no longer focusing on the disappointing football game.

I noticed how smoking numbed my internal pain that night, so I smoked, and I smoked, and I smoked for many years thereafter. When the effects of the marijuana failed to numb my inner pain, I chose harder drugs.

I would do almost anything to make the pain deep inside go away.

Message From The Universe:

Throughout life, a person can lessen the pain caused from any particular experience by using different forms of pain relief. The types of pain relief available to humans are as numerous as the causes of pain. Whether a person chooses drugs or exercise, sex or video games, it does not matter so long as they don't forget who they are, what caused their pain, and why they are here.

Things were a little different when I was young. It was normal for kids from the block to get together during the weekends and go riding dirt bikes out in the desert, which was right down the street from my childhood home. I had four friends who would always head out into the desert with me to go riding. In the desert, we built a riding trail and even created a fort to hang out in since most of the time the sun was scorching hot. It was our own home away from home. There was only one rule: "No girls allowed in our desert fort!"

One day while I was riding my dirt bike in the desert, I came across a pornographic magazine. At first, like many young boys, I was grossed out by the pictures and illustrations. Sadly, when I turned thirteen, pornography became a teacher and a friend.

My parents were embarrassed by human sexuality and believed it had no place in their home. As devoutly religious people, they refused to take any active role in my sexual education. They were caught up in the model of "If you get a girl pregnant, don't bring that whore and that bastard child to my house." So, any questions I had regarding sex were completely ignored by my parents.

They were under the ridiculous belief that if you ignored your child's development, all the issues related to sexual urges would magically disappear. Unfortunately, my sexual urges never went away, and since I had no guidance about my sexual feelings, my sexuality became a destructive force.

As a child, I craved *Love* and understanding, but what I experienced was judgment and abuse. One day, when I was thirteen, a neighborhood girl told me to come by her house to hang out when her parents were gone. I waited anxiously by my window for them to leave. Once they did, I ran over to her house and jumped over the back wall to meet her. She invited me in, and we had sex. Yes, I lost my virginity when I was thirteen.

It was wonderful! I felt alive and wanted. I experienced being one with another person and the feeling of creation. No, she did not get pregnant, but this newfound experience began to fuel my existence. Yes, I wanted to have sex every day and all the time. It didn't matter with whom, or when; all that mattered was that I felt wanted and cherished.

In all the animalistic responses associated with sex and the satisfaction associated with intercourse, I felt like I was good for something. I thought sex was *Love.* The harder, longer, and more deviant sex became over the years, the more satisfying it felt. The reality is, having sex and being *Loved* are two distinct and completely different experiences.

Let's take a look back and examine some of the events that changed and helped shape who I had become. As a teen, I associated drugs with pain relief and confused *Love* for sex. By the time I was in college, it was party all evening and have sex all night. Then I became a junior partner at a big-time law firm. The more money I made, the more sex and drugs penetrated my life. Because they made me feel better about myself, I became addicted to these physical desires, and I was always trying to satisfy my new addictions. This scenario played out for me hundreds of times.

For me, it was all about sex, drugs, and rock 'n' roll. The more sex I had, the better I felt about myself. The more drugs I consumed, the less pain I felt. It was a vicious cycle where I was destroying myself and others. Yet, I felt liberated because I believed I had solved the difficulties of my own existence with sex and drugs.

Wow, what a mind-blowing discovery. I was one of many using this destructive formula to try to resolve pain and agony. I wish I could tell you these two components completely eliminated my pain and allowed me to become a wonderful person who was a contributing member of society. That would be a lie because these two unbridled desires nearly killed me.

Message From The Universe:

Every form of refuge has its price.

Soon after leaving the district attorney's office, I got married to a wonderful woman from the Midwest named Edna. About eight years into my marriage, I started having extramarital affairs. Edna and I had dated for about ten years before we got married. You know the saying, "A slice of pepperoni pizza every day makes pizza boring." Since sex offered validation, I needed to find more sex to fill the hole in my heart. Unfortunately, I never found enough sex to fill that hole. In actuality, the more sex I had, the bigger the void became.

Why couldn't I fill the hole in my heart? I was hurting everyone in my life, including myself. First, I was lying to my wife and children about where I was going and what I was doing. Second, I was lying to the people I was attempting to seduce. Last, I was causing heartache and pain by ghosting (ignoring them, disappearing from their lives) the other women once I had my fun.

Once I was done chasing sex on any particular day, the search for drugs to numb my pain began. Simply stated, life in general is harder when you do drugs. When you don't do drugs, you simply finish work and go about your business having fun with your family and friends. You don't have to make up lies, you don't lose sleep, it doesn't cost a fortune, and you don't worry constantly about getting caught. When you do drugs, you have to find the drugs. Then you have to sneak off to find a place to do the drugs. When you find the drugs, you have to pay for them. When you do the drugs, you have to find a place to hang out because you can't be around your family or your true friends while under the influence.

When you finally get home from doing all the partying, you have to lie about the entire experience. You don't want to look your family members in their eyes since you look and smell horrible. You act offended when those who truly care for you ask questions about where you have been and with whom you have been hanging out.

The whole time you are just looking for a way to grab what you need to get right back out on the street so you can start the destructive partying behavior all over again. You then storm up the stairs and lock yourself in your room, isolating yourself from society until you can make a break for the door to get out of your perceived prison. Yes, in this scenario, the drugs turn your sanctuary, your family, and your home into a perceived prison, and the drugs turn the streets into your new friend. You have basically traded away your home and family to be on the streets so you can party all the time.

Drug use is a vicious cycle full of lies, full of pain, and full of disgust from beginning to end. I was trying to fill the void in my heart with the same darkness that had created the void in the first place. My life was lies and deceit. I was trying to create a false reality of being a wonderful husband and a great father while running away from my family all night long and returning home broke and looking like I had been hit by a freight train. The darkness involved in the act of using drugs shadows the light of your existence, and you are never truly recognized for who and what you are. Drug use as a solution never works since the opposing forces in the experience eventually cancel themselves out, and you are back to square one with a heavy heart and overwhelming sadness.

My first few affairs started as simple rendezvous, but one day, I met a Southern belle who was a ballerina and a headliner on the Las Vegas strip. The night I met her, I was out with my friends, and we all had a wonderful evening together. We played until six in the morning; then I ran home to be husband and a father. Since I made all the money, I thought I could do whatever I wanted. I thought I had sacrificed and suffered so much that I decided I just wanted to play,

play, and play. I bought into the old cliché "What she doesn't know will not hurt her." I thought I was getting away with murder, but actually, I was killing myself and destroying my family.

Edna always knew somewhere deep down what I was up to. It is like she had a sixth sense. But when she sensed a disturbance in the relationship, she simply retreated into her shell as a protective mechanism. It was almost as if she were saying, "If I don't see it, then it won't hurt," or better yet, "I am giving him the benefit of the doubt." This allowed Edna to shift her focus to more important responsibilities like raising the children or going to work. As often happens, it gave me a lot of leeway when it came to explaining how I spent my time. The more withdrawn Edna became, the more I played, the less I came home, and the farther apart we grew. Eventually, as they say, give a man enough rope and he will hang himself, or better, he will hang the marriage. One day, the benefit of the doubt was gone and Edna became the judge, jury, and executioner. When that happened, my begging for mercy fell upon deaf ears.

I must say Edna was no square. For a while, she liked partying some, but after we purchased a home and our second child was on the way, she settled down. One late evening, she looked into my eyes and said, "Honey, you're going down a road I cannot go down. Please don't go down that road. It will destroy you."

You would think I would listen to the warning. Oh, hell no! I said to myself. I got this all figured out. I know what I need, and I can get it anytime I want. Everything else will fall into place.

What I should have known was that this road was a dead end leading only to the complete destruction of myself.

Like so many functioning alcoholics and addicts, I always made my client appointments and court appearances. I was very serious about my law practice, but I wasn't serious about my personal life.

Then, one day, I decided to leave my home and family for the Southern belle—we were going to have the time of our lives.

Message From The Universe:

> A relationship born in the darkness will never successfully exist outside of the darkness—it can never survive in the light. Eventually, everyone is seen in the light.

I separated from my wonderful wife and my two beautiful infants in a blaze of glory, like a shooting star. One of the beautiful things about a shooting star is how brightly it lights the night sky. The sad part about a shooting star is how fast it burns out. Well, I had just become that proverbial shooting star blazing across the sky! I headed out of my home and rented a luxurious penthouse suite, which was approximately 3,200 square feet and overlooked the strip. This building only had nine units, and all of the residents were successful, single males. Can you imagine the parties?

I would come home at 6 a.m. with a car full of people after clubbing all night long to find the building full of people partying on every floor and dancing on the balconies. The nights were long, and the action was fierce. Then one day, I noticed my ring finger looked like a rutabaga. It was swollen, puss was coming out the sides, and it was incredibly painful. I went to the emergency room where the doctor told me I had contracted Methicillin-resistant Staphylococcus Aureus (MRSA).

MRSA is a nasty, fleshing-eating bacteria that can be found on any part of the body, typically on the skin, but it is usually destroyed by your immune system. After examining my finger, the doctor gave me a prescription and told me to take it easy for a while so my finger could heal. The doctor's words went in one ear and came right out of the other. I was like, "If it doesn't kill you, it makes you stronger." I left that emergency department stronger that day, so the party bus rolled on.

A few weeks later, I began having high fevers, chills, and night sweats, coupled with extreme weight loss. In a month, I went to the emergency room five times. During that same period, I went from 192 pounds to 152. I had lost more than forty pounds in thirty days. My pants no longer fit and my suits were falling off. For a second, I believed it was the famous "Las Vegas Diet," but deep down inside, I knew better.

Later, I found out it was a terminal illness. I also found out I had a very short time to live.

On October 18, 2012, I was diagnosed with an incurable, terminal disease. The hospital called my cell phone while I was grocery shopping. I was supposed to have the kids at my penthouse for the next three days. I recognized the number, so I took the call. I expected to hear I had the flu, and I was physically fine, but that wasn't even close.

A medical technician asked, "Are you Luis?" I said, "Yes." What he said next rocked my world. "You are very sick. In fact, you are terminally ill and must contact your personal physician immediately." The room started to spin, and I sat down in the middle of the grocery store. The only thing I could process was, "I am dying." I began to think of my daughters who were three and four at the time. I could not hold back the tears, so I sat there and cried like a baby.

I didn't cry for me—I cried for them. I cried about how I had not been around much, and when I was around, my focus was not on them. I cried about how I had treated Edna, and I cried about how I had just gotten up one day and left my family. I cried because I was going to be leaving my family behind with so much sadness, grief, and loss. We all know how hard it is to raise kids. Can you imagine raising two girls as a single parent while working a full-time job?

What did I do as I sat there with the whole world spinning around me? I called the one person I had always *Loved*. I called Edna.

At that moment, I knew the affair was over, and I thought my *Love* was also over. See, splitting up and filing for divorce is traumatic. But having your spouse return with an incurable, terminal illness after running around partying and having affairs—well, let's just say that was like dropping a bomb on Edna.

Fortunately, our relationship was founded on *Love*. As a registered nurse, Edna immediately sent me to the right medical facility where they were able to control the deadly disease. Today, thanks to Edna and the medical providers, I am completely cured and healthy as a horse.

And the Southern belle? She did not *Love* me. She was infatuated by my job and my success. The minute the dynamics of our conditional relationship changed, she was gone. When I told her I was sick, she never spoke to me again.

Message From The Universe:

Love at first sight truly exists and is one of the most powerful forces in the Universe. The power it generates can change a person's course. Do not underestimate the power of love at first sight.

Summers in the Midwest are warm and humid. I don't know if you have ever experienced a summer day in Illinois, but the temperature can be as high as ninety-two degrees with 80 percent humidity. What does that feel like? Put it this way—if you take a cold shower to cool down from the heat, you begin sweating the minute you turn the shower off.

Back in 1995, I had just returned to Chicago to start my final year of law school. A couple of my buddies decided to go have a few beers to cool off, so I joined them. I did not know it was going to be one of the most monumental days of my life. As I stood there in the crowded pub, I caught a glimpse of a beautiful blond. She was about 5' 4", with a gorgeous figure, and the most beautiful blue eyes I had ever seen.

I said to myself, "If I had a chance with such a beautiful woman, I would marry her in a second." I prayed for an opportunity to talk to her. All of a sudden, my wish came true. As she was leaving, she walked right by me. I jumped in front of her and shouted in her face, "Hey what's your name?" Once she gave me her name, I asked if I could call her. As she continued walking to exit, she looked at me and said, "Look me up. I'm in the phone book." I thought that was the first and last time I would ever see this beautiful woman.

All the way home, I beat myself up about how I could have done better. I was saddened by how badly I had approached her and depressed we had not had an opportunity to talk. I even convinced myself she had given me a fake name. Discouraged, I didn't write her name down, and by morning, I had no idea what it was.

Fortunately, I had the smartest guy in my law school class sitting right next to me when she shouted her name. The next morning, my roommate and I joined our buddies for breakfast. My friends asked if I had called the beautiful woman with the blue eyes. I laughed and said, "No. She was probably playing with me, and anyway, I don't even remember her name." That's when my luck showed up to help me out. My smart friend, the one with an eidetic memory, shouted out her name—Edna Brinkly—and spelled it for me. It was almost like a scene in a movie. When I got home, I grabbed the phone book, and to my surprise, her name and number were in the white pages.

I called Edna. Of course, I called her. She was the most beautiful girl I had ever seen. She had a phenomenal aura that radiated white light. And she immediately remembered me. I was shocked anyone could remember me since I had been such a disappointment all my life.

She actually said, "I was hoping you would call." It made me feel wonderful.

Edna and I made plans to go to dinner and a movie the next evening. We dated for ten years before we got married. If I had to do it all over again, I would have never made her wait so long. I should have married her shortly after I met her. It hurt her to wait all those years. It also hurt her to see me leave her for someone else. Eventually, because of my actions, her trust and respect for me died. After twenty-eight years together, we divorced and went our separate ways.

And it hurt her to see me so sick when I returned home.

I can't blame Edna for moving away from me after all the hurt and pain I had caused her. I will always be thankful for the moments we spent together and for the lessons she taught me. For her sincere *Love* for me, she was despised by my parents and ridiculed by her family during our marriage. Many of her friends stopped speaking to her because they could not understand her unbridled *Love* for me.

People can dislike you for who you are and for who you are not. In our situation, they didn't understand our non-judgmental and unyielding *Love*. They didn't understand that *Love* is about supporting a person when they are hurt, when they are down, or when they are lost. *Love* is not about kicking someone to the curb when they are going through difficult times. *Love* is about telling someone, "Come home and be with us," instead of slamming the door in their face.

See, Edna had always been showered in *Love*. Her parents were farmers, and although she wanted a career in nursing, her parents did not attack her for wanting to be different. Quite the opposite—her parents encouraged her to be what she wanted to be and told her she could achieve anything through hard work and perseverance. They provided her with a foundation to succeed, or better said, they provided her with the foundation to take off. Her parents instilled the courage and fortitude to move forward in whatever direction she wanted.

One of the greatest lessons Edna learned she learned from her mother at a very young age. One day, her mother took her aside and said, "I will always *Love* you no matter what you do, but always know that I will never lie for you." I believe this statement reinforced for Edna that her mother's *Love* was unshakable, but it also made her understand she had to take responsibility for her actions and not lie. Once a parent begins to lie for a child, the child begins to believe lying is okay. Typically, it is difficult to break the habit once you start lying and shifting blame onto others. The inability to take responsibility for your action creates a false reality, which can end in total destruction.

Sure, Edna's family had open discussions about her behavior, but they never made her feel like she was no good or less than. Quite simply, she was never judged or condemned by her family. To make a child feel like they are no good, or less than, is to make them believe they are unsalvageable. When we believe we are unsalvageable, we lose faith in ourselves and humanity. Often, individuals who believe this way about themselves eliminate all higher thinking and replace it with instinctive thoughts and behaviors.

What does that mean? If you want something, steal it. If someone gets in your way, destroy them. If you want sex, you just take it. The dignity for human life and respect for others is eliminated from the thought process and replaced with selfishness. So, if they break someone's heart, they do not care. If they take someone's wallet, they don't care, and if they break someone's arm, they don't care. This sociopathic behavior then becomes a way of survival for the individual where they become a destructive force in others' lives, leaving a wake of destruction.

Message From The Universe:

The truth always comes out in the end.

What people should understand is that the darkness observes when you are in pain, and then it asks you to turn off your little night-light so it can consume you. This happens around the world millions upon millions of times on any given day. Once you turn off your little night-light, the darkness tells you that you can find happiness in things like lying, committing crimes, doing drugs, having uncontrolled sex, or simply hurting others.

In reality, no happiness can be found in any of these actions—they only cause you to drift further from your true self. At some point, you will regret your actions. Then you will do something you thought you would never do. You'll lie so no one finds out what you did, but you will not be any happier. Deep down, you will actually be more depressed and sadder about your new level of existence.

Message From The Universe:

There is no happiness in the darkness, just more sadness.

You are in more pain since you can't believe you just did that horrible act, whatever it might be, and you can't get it out of your conscious mind. So where do you put it? You put it straight into the treasure box called your subconscious mind. For a while, you get tunnel vision, and you forget what you did and whom you hurt. But the darkness won't let you forget. It does not apologize or give you good advice because its sole mission is to consume you. It tries to convince you things didn't go your way because you weren't vicious enough, you did not lie enough, you were not underhanded enough.

Now, if your life is guided by these factors and you attempt to understand the experiences, you can't because it is completely irrational. The reality is you are killing yourself. You are uncontrollably spinning internally and the balance in your life is gone. At this point, many jump right back into the dark behavior and go out to find someone else to victimize. When we sober up, we find ourselves back at square one. Just remember, we all have pain, and we all just want to be *Loved.* In the darkness, we lose sight of our life's mission, and we lose sight of ourselves.

For the few moments we are sober, we talked about the person we used to be and the people we used to *Love,* forgetting that once upon a time, we *Loved* ourselves. In all this sadness of losing ourselves, many of us will intentionally overdose or allow ourselves to become very ill so all the pain will just go away as quickly as possible. We become so lost that we don't see the little night-light sitting right in front of us shouting, "Let me help you!"

My mission in this life is writing this book, which I offer to all people regardless of ethnicity, race, gender, sexual orientation/identity, or color. I always knew I would eventually write. The problem was my life was so out of control that something had to make me hit the brakes or I was going to fail at my mission. Simply put, my life had become too heavy to continue.

Then I realized all the pain from the crashes in my life made me sober up and get back to my real mission, which is to help others. Throughout, I remembered I was a good person who was here to help others. In the end, I thanked the Universe for my shortcomings, as they were what encouraged me to write this book.

If I can do it, then anyone can do it. I have faith in you! All it takes is to turn on your little night-light and let the light of this existence shine into your life. It does not have to be a monumental change where you walk away from everything—just a little change at a time.

Start by eliminating lying. By simply changing the bearing of your life slightly, you will create a new trajectory where the sky is the limit. You will create a path where you can begin to forgive yourself for the things you did, but also you can accept the things you did as they have brought you to a new, wonderful realization. For me, all the pain has fueled me to write about my experiences so others suffer less, so others are less judgmental of themselves, and so others are not so manipulated by the darkness.

So, wherever you are, turn on your little night-light! Know that I *Love* you, and I am sitting here with you through this long night. I understand your pain, and I know you can fight through the darkness into the light. Then you can *Love* again.

> "Success is not final. Failure is not fatal.
> It is the courage to continue that counts."
>
> — Winston Churchill

Suggested listening: *Oh Very Young* by Cat Stevens

Chapter 11

Goodbye My Love

"We are all broken, that is how the light gets in."

— Ernest Hemingway

I now come to a close. I wonder what life would be like if I hadn't gone down this path. Who would I be? Where would I be? How would I feel? The words I shared with you brought me here with you today, drawing *us* a little closer to our truth. I wish for you, my dear friend, to follow up and seek the answers to your deepest questions. I know you have many questions. I wish I had all the answers, but then life wouldn't be a mystery—it would be a bore.

As I continue with my own journey, I realize this is just the beginning. I have many more choices and many more doors to open and venture through. As I ponder the trials and tribulations of my deepest questions and the forthcoming answers, I will always appreciate all the roads I have traveled. Some roads were long, hard, and seemed to have no end. But even the darkest path has led me to this beautiful place where I sit here with you. I will always cherish our time together. The tears and the laughter are all part of the same road home. You on your journey and I am on mine.

Many amazing thought leaders encourage us to stay in the present moment so we will never feel scared, afraid, or less than. As for me, I will always keep safe some of my darkest memories because they are a gentle reminder of where I have been and what led me here to you. Whether it was a disagreement with my wife or an argument with my family, I choose not to wallow in dark memories. Instead, I allow them to bounce off my radar, and I quickly remind myself, "Don't go there." Perhaps you can keep this in your thoughts when you find yourself rapidly heading down the slippery slope of a repeated experience that seems to get you nowhere fast.

On a day when you are feeling down and out, when the world seems to be stomping on your forehead without concern for your wellbeing, please remember I care for your wellbeing. If you look around, other people also care about your wellbeing. At first, you may only find one person who can see you, who can hear you, and who can give you some good old Vitamin-TLC (tender loving care). So, don't be shy, don't be conceited or pretentious; reach out and touch someone by acknowledging them with kind words or by giving them a big smile. All these free acts of kindness help to develop a bond of caring between people. Open the door for someone, whether or not they need the help.

Did I ever mention how fulfilling helping others can be? By lending an ear, or giving another person a little time, or putting forth some affection toward a person in pain, you may learn a valuable lesson about yourself. The Universe puts people, places, and things in our lives so we may learn about our special attributes. The information then downloads into our psyche to allow us more information when we are making our next set of decisions.

Message From The Universe:

You never stop making decisions!

Life is an endless menu of choices with common questions like what to eat, what to wear, what to say, and what to do being asked continuously. You met me, and I took you through some specific events in my life. You now understand the impressions those events made on me, molding the middle-aged man I am today. Did I make wrong choices? I cannot say my choices were wrong. What I can say is I made my choices, and I lived through my consequences. That is called taking responsibility for your decisions and accepting your actions. At every level, I was consciously involved in the events through the choices I made. These consequences brought me much of life's fearful derivatives, such as sadness and despair. Yet, I can honestly say I would not be here with you had I not made those choices.

Message From The Universe:

Just because you suffer from your choices does not mean you made the wrong decision.

Remember, everyone has their own level of tolerance for pain. Only you know how much pain you can endure. Edna always told me I was as strong as an ox. Well, let's just say I had a high tolerance for pain that I consciously chose to impose upon myself through the choices I made. I have told Edna over and over for the last couple of years, "There is no happiness in the darkness." That is one phrase I hope you will recall if you begin to slip back down that slope and into your old ways.

Stop! Do not go there! You will always have the same result from a dark experience. Did you not learn from your first dark experience? If you did not learn your lesson, don't worry, and don't beat yourself up or let others beat you up. Simply understand that you will experience the same result from that dark decision over and over until you learn your lesson. Eventually, you will get it, but if you don't, the Universe will step in and try to help you out by sending various types of help. Typically, we call these "problems." Whether it is the loss of your money, or the loss of your health, or the loss of your job, it is all happening to send you a message.

I wrote this book about what I believe are the different aspects of *Love*. *Love* is the opposite of the darkness. What is the beast I keep referring to as the "darkness"? It is a feeling, an energy, a thought that can attack you when you least expect it. When you are not protected and when you have your guard down, it comes upon you to destroy you and those around you. We see and experience this energy daily because it is all around us. We can never escape it, but we must never succumb to it.

The darkness can manifest itself within each of us if we are not careful. Some of us do not even recognize it is literally running our lives. The darkness and its energy can be seen as greed, envy, ridicule, and judgment. It can also be experienced as depression, anger, arguments, lies, and manipulation. It can be acts of cruelty upon others such as a smirk, rolling your eyes, gossip, or even silence. Other forms of darkness include alcohol abuse, drug abuse, neglect, child abuse, hurting yourself (cutting), pornography, name calling, bullying, or laying your hands upon another human being with the intent to hurt them. Let's not forget war. These actions are not in the scope of the practice of *Love.*

Just understand that you are not bad because you have chosen to experience these dark energies. Realize you are a being of the light, and as such, you will never, ever find happiness in the darkness. Now, I encourage you to stop for a moment and listen to the all-encompassing silence of *Love.* In that space ask yourself, "Why am I here?" Ask yourself, "What caused me to seek this experience?" Ask yourself, "What led me down this road time after time?" And ask yourself, "Why am I using the darkness to cover up my light?" We all remember, once upon a time, when we resonated *Love.* Your answers will show you the road back home.

Today, move toward *Love.* It will begin to heal some of your pain and will allow you to recognize the *Love* always around you. In this healing, you can begin again to *Love* yourself, and then down the road, you can begin to *Love* others. With this newfound direction, you will begin to experience forgiveness, compassion, kindness, and acceptance. You will vibrate *Love*, causing the vibration of those around you to go up. Then, we humans can function as one big family in the space of *Love.*

In this space, we will all act as one for we all *Love* one another. In this space, our differences are welcomed, and our uniqueness is appreciated. In this space, acts of abuse and violence are nonexistent and unnecessary. It is a space where the student is valued as much as the teacher, and the child is valued as much as the parent. It is a space where everyone is seen as an equal and cherished for their individuality. In this space, peace and happiness among people is seen as a foundation made of solid rock, which is indestructible, unshakable, unmovable, and supports our humanity. Without a doubt, I can tell you the answer is *Love*.

"This lifetime will never come again; it is precious and irreplaceable. To live without regret, we must have a concrete purpose, continually setting goals and challenges for ourselves. And we need to keep moving toward those specific targets steadily and tenaciously, one step at a time."

— Daisaku Ikeda

Suggested listening: *Lean on Me* by Bill Withers

Chapter 12

Affirmations
(55 Insights)

"I know for sure that what we dwell on is what we become."

— Oprah Winfrey

Throughout this book, you have read certain words and phrases given to me by the Universe. To me, these words and phrases come from a distinct, audible voice that I hear and that has been with me since I was a child. You know the voice I am talking about. It is the same voice that told you not to put your finger in the flame or put your hand into the blender. I remember distinctly hearing this voice when I was about to sign the papers for the short sale of my home. As I sat there, I heard a voice say, "Don't do this!" Well, in my arrogance, I signed the sale documents. I paid dearly.

I have gathered all the Universal sayings from this book and provided them here for you as a quick guide to help you during your "Road of Life." I hope these quotes help you understand your road a little better and also help you understand the stop signs along the way so you can complete your mission.

Go get 'em tiger!

UNIVERSE: You are made of the same materials as the stars and planets. In your universal consciousness you carry with you the ability to know the universal truths. The truth has a distinct vibration and feeling. The birth of a child is grand, as are mountains, oceans, and stars, in the perspective of the glory of the Universe. There is nothing more beautiful in the Universe than to see another human being truly happy. This is to experience the vibration of love physically, emotionally, and spiritually. It was this love that created the Universe. You did not make a fool of yourself.

UNIVERSE: Love is a state of being. It comes from knowing your place in the Universe and being at peace with the equality of all things. It is through this understanding of equality that the soul becomes satisfied and can resonate happiness through the self and onto others. This vibrational resonance is called love. Love is the law of the Universe. Love is always present in the space of now. As the basic and main building block to our existence, it is the glue that keeps this reality together. It is incredibly underestimated, but it is highly contagious to human beings if allowed to develop. In the alternative, the ego fights against equality through judgment, therefore spawning prosecution, persecution, and competition between human beings.

UNIVERSE: Acceptance is love in motion. Through acceptance, you acknowledge the circumstances and those involved, but you do not judge either the participants or the events. By accepting the event in its entirety, you see how the event serves you and how the event serves in the growth of all involved. Everything is all good for everyone!

UNIVERSE: Guilt is an emotional response caused by fear. Specifically, it is the fear of being unloved, unworthy, or less than others. It is a fear-driven response in which you believe you are not acceptable because of your behavior, your thoughts, your condition, or your consequences. Within this suspected flaw, you believe you are no longer equal to the rest of humanity. When guilt is internalized, it lowers your vibrational state. It is an illusion and not recognized by the Universe. Unfortunately, the person imposing the guilt generally believes they are helping or enlightening you. You must protect yourself from guilt!

UNIVERSE: Remember you are a rightful member of this great and vast Universe. Regardless of how you were created, you are here now. Therefore, it is your birthright to experience all the choices you manifest. Specifically, you have the right to experience all the possible outcomes from the choices you make. But I must warn you, be careful because dire consequences can stem directly from your choices. See, you have the right to make the choices, but when you do, you own the decision and have earned the consequences. Regardless of the outcomes, every experience serves the universal purpose of enlightenment. Love is the law of the Universe.

UNIVERSE: The answer is love.

UNIVERSE: Hereditary pain is the pain inherited from generation to generation. It is pain caused by some form of perceived guilt, which is internalized over the years in the subconscious mind. Adults transfer the guilt to their children or relatives when a similar experience arises. At that moment, the pain and suffering of many generations can be transposed onto a child or relative through guilt. This guilt then makes the person feel unloved, unworthy, and lesser than.

UNIVERSE: Violence in any form used upon another human being violates the rules of creation and is completely unacceptable. This physical force destroys a human being's love, a human being's confidence, and a human being's self-worth. Whether through words or through actions, violence will never solve a problem since it only creates pain and hurt for the perpetrator and the recipient.

UNIVERSE: Although the book of life is different for each person, the one thing guaranteed to all people is suffering. While some suffering is dealt with immediately by the conscious mind and released, other events may take years to be addressed. Whichever road the person takes is fine, so long as they understand it must be dealt with at some point. Upon dealing with the event that caused the suffering, the energy you are using to hold onto the experience and the energy the Universe is using to keep the memories of the event in your mind, heart, and soul are released. These memories then simply start to flow away on the eternal river of forgiveness.

UNIVERSE: Humans have evolved to the level of understanding right and wrong at a very young age. But we still have to teach our children to identify "wrong" behavior or they may develop destructive attitudes, causing drastic consequences. As a parent, you are molding your child into what they become. The manner of molding a child is intricately important to your child's future success. If you treat your child like an animal, don't be surprised if they grow up to be an animal.

UNIVERSE: Only the darkness deals in absolutes because it is void of understanding, patience, or compassion.

UNIVERSE: No one can control the Universe. In its magnanimous glory, its energy is always in control, and its energy is always directed toward the light of love. Those who attempt to control the Universe will always fall short because the energy of the Universe is unlimited.

UNIVERSE: Stop the unkindness. Unkindness is used to transfer suffering onto another. People may believe that through their unkind actions, they may release their suffering, without consequence, and their suffering will stop. Sadly, the transfer of suffering is usually from an adult to a child, since children's resistance is typically minimal. It does not eliminate a person's suffering; it only causes more suffering for the unkind person and causes suffering for the recipient of the unkind act. So just simply stop being unkind!

UNIVERSE: Respect cannot be forced by another; it can only be earned. Respect is normally earned through acts of compassion, understanding, and love. These are the basic building blocks of respect.

UNIVERSE: Time heals all wounds.

UNIVERSE: Love always starts with the individual first loving themselves and then loving others. If a person cannot love themselves, they truly don't understand how to love, and they will have difficulty loving others. It is through our practice of love that all battles are won.

UNIVERSE: Only great love defeats great hate.

UNIVERSE: Children are thinking machines. They are unique in that they are more observant than adults. Children listen for many years before speaking. In doing all that listening, children develop the ability to hear the message sent through a person's acts and through a person's heart.

UNIVERSE: Love unifies all people through its respect for the dignity of all life regardless of race, age, religion, ethnicity, sexual identity, or condition. As a unifying force, love creates a vibration where we can accept ourselves and others. On this equal playing field, we can all have open dialogue without judgment.

UNIVERSE: Love comes from the feeling of equality found in any particular experience. Every experience is comprised of a specific cause and a subsequent effect that someday is manifested. Once you see all of the possible outcomes with humbleness and humility for having the experience, you begin to feel the unconditional love found in the totality of the circumstances. This acceptance for all the possible outcomes is where unconditional love resides, and the ego is not welcomed.

UNIVERSE: Once you let go of the ego, you will know who you truly are. Once you know who you truly are, your responses will be based on love, not on conditions or expectations.

UNIVERSE: Conditional love is a label given to the mistaken belief that people can only be cherished, accepted, and truly appreciated if they achieve certain behaviors, certain accomplishments, or a certain status. It is the first step in creating inequality between people and is a destructive force.

UNIVERSE: Everything has a beginning, and everything has an end; there are no exceptions to this rule.

UNIVERSE: Sometimes the farther away things seem, the closer they really are.

UNIVERSE: There is resolution in the silence. Silence is a significant part of reflection. In that reflection we can see the happiness that existed once upon a time. In that space, we can truly appreciate our experiences.

UNIVERSE: Time stops for no one. The past cannot be changed, but humans have the ability to change the future. As our intentions change so does our future. If we want a desired outcome, we must change our intentions—that will create the desired effect.

UNIVERSE: Anyone who believes there is a hierarchy in wrongness does not understand the Universe. When you're wrong, you're wrong; that is it! It is where the introspective analysis ends. It is not offset because of your past actions or your potential future acts. There are no levels of wrong.

UNIVERSE: Perspective is everything. It is the embodiment of reflection.

UNIVERSE: The truth always finds a way.

UNIVERSE: Intention is very important to our existence as humans. It fuels a person's willpower. When a person's intention and willpower are aligned with their mission, they can move mountains.

UNIVERSE: The Universe is one, and you are one with the Universe. Although you may be a member of this planet, you do not have to incorporate the negative emotions of this planet into your life.

UNIVERSE: The destruction of another person's life through murder or by any other means is a travesty of monumental consequences. To destroy the life of another human being as a means of obtaining a specific purpose is not found in any religious dogma or supported by any rational thought. It is strictly a creation of the ego and fueled by a person's emotions.

UNIVERSE: For every action, there is a registered effect, a reaction. You will experience all the effects of every action you create when the variables needed for you to understand the experience are ripe.

UNIVERSE: Narcissism is the effect of extremely self-centered acts on a person's identity, relationships, and life. It is an illusion created by the mind, fueled by the ego, and played out through selfish acts and intentions of a person who seems to destroy others while exalting the self.

UNIVERSE: Humanity is always struggling for perfection. In this present existence, within this dimension, no person, place, or thing is perfect. That's the rule!

UNIVERSE: Perfection exists in the Universe, but it is not as most people define it. The perfection of the Universe exists in the differences found between ourselves and other people, places, and things. Many believe perfection can only exist in one idea or belief system. The perfection of the Universe lies in the actual differences between all the enumerated beliefs, ideas, and systems. It is this randomness in everything, in every occurrence and in everyone, that is the order of the Universe.

UNIVERSE: Only great love conquers great hate.

UNIVERSE: Compassion is love through reflection. When you step into the shoes of another person, you recognize their existence and acknowledge their circumstances. You understand their pain and thereby reflect their pain onto yourself. This creates an understanding of the experiences of another. It creates mutual respect for the human condition in each individual.

UNIVERSE: Your birth into this existence makes you worthy to receive and enjoy all the wonderful gifts bestowed upon you without guilt or regret. You earned what you received—deserve has nothing to do with it.

UNIVERSE: Don't overthink life. It is what it is, and that is all that it is.

UNIVERSE: All requests are heard. A request to help others is the intention of love put into action. If made with a sincere heart with no expectation of gain, all the forces in the Universe will align to help achieve the desired result.

UNIVERSE: Upon being born, every human being owes a death. Death is a function of life. Both birth and death operate jointly as an experience of life, which motivates humans to grow during their lifetimes. Most people believe death only happens once in their lifetime. Yet, death, like rebirth, is happening constantly throughout a person's existence.

UNIVERSE: Most people view problems as negative experiences that only create suffering and pain. In actuality, your problems are there to liberate you from the things holding you back. You should celebrate your problems because in their truth you will be set free.

UNIVERSE: Every person has a mission to complete during their life that is directly tied to the further enlightenment of their being. Although each mission is different for each person, this mission is the single most important happening of that person's life. A person's whole existence is in tune with their mission from the day of their birth.

UNIVERSE: Love always starts with loving oneself. Once people love themselves, they can love others.

UNIVERSE: What you feel in your heart engulfs your thoughts. Your thoughts dictate your actions. Your actions create your reality. Your reality creates what you feel in your heart. This is the circle of life.

UNIVERSE: Faith is the belief that a person can and will transcend any obstacle they encounter and the understanding that all roads lead home.

UNIVERSE: Throughout life, a person can lessen the pain caused from any particular experience by using different forms of pain relief. The types of pain relief available to humans are as numerous as the causes of pain. Whether a person chooses drugs or exercise, sex or video games, it does not matter so long as they don't forget who they are, what caused their pain, and why they are here.

UNIVERSE: Every form of refuge has its price.

UNIVERSE: A relationship born in the darkness will never successfully exist outside of the darkness—it can never survive in the light. Eventually, everyone is seen in the light.

UNIVERSE: Love at first sight truly exists and is one of the most powerful forces in the Universe. The power it generates can change a person's course. Do not underestimate the power of love at first sight.

UNIVERSE: The truth always comes out in the end.

UNIVERSE: There is no happiness in the darkness, just more sadness.

UNIVERSE: You never stop making decisions!

UNIVERSE: Just because you suffer from your choices does not mean you made the wrong decision.

"I always feel happy. You know why? Because I don't expect anything from anyone. Expectations always hurt. Life is short. So, love your life. Be happy and keep smiling. Just live for yourself and before you speak, listen. Before you write, think. Before you spend, earn. Before you pray, forgive. Before you hurt, feel. Before you hate, love. Before you quit, try. Before you die, live."

— Author Unknown

Suggested listening: *End of the Line* by The Traveling Wilburys

Goodbye My Love

by Luis J. Rojas

The day will come with no reprieve

Where I must say goodbye and leave

For me I'll sit and ponder on

About the loves now lost and gone

A million thanks to those who were

Moments I cherished and did not deserve

Tomorrow will come and roll on by

At night I'll sit and watch the sky

What I know now deep in my heart

Is that my love for you will never part

So as my book comes to an end

Always remember you were my friend

The End

About the Author

LUIS ROJAS was born in Miami, Florida, to Cuban immigrants. His family ethnicity includes French, Spaniard, Cuban, and Sicilian. He obtained a Bachelor of Arts in Criminal Justice from the University of Nevada-Reno. Then he earned a Doctorate of Juris Prudence from Drake University in 1992.

Luis' first job in the legal system was as an appeal clerk for the Clark County District Attorney's office. After being admitted to practice law by the Supreme Court of the State of Nevada in 1993, he began prosecuting criminals for misdemeanor and felony offenses. During this time, he became a member of the National District Attorney's Association and was acknowledged by the Fraternity of Desert Big Horn for significant contributions to the conservation and welfare of the Desert Big Horn Sheep.

Luis left the District Attorney's Office in 1997 to practice criminal law in the private sector. In 1999, he became a partner of renowned criminal defense attorney Stephen Stein. Together, they formed the Law Office of Stein and Rojas, which faithfully served the residents of Las Vegas, Nevada, for more than fifteen years.

During his practice as a criminal defense attorney, Luis was recognized as a member in good standing of the Nevada Trial Lawyers Association and the Association of Trial Lawyers of America. In 2004, he was listed as a member in the National Register's *Who's Who in Executives and Professionals*. In 2006, he was recognized by The Shade Tree Sheltering Women and Children for making a difference. In 2012, Luis received a Certificate of Appointment issued by the Nevada Supreme Court as a mentor in the State Bar of Nevada's Mentorship Program.

Presently, Luis serves as a private business and legal consultant to Biologix, LLC. He is also an inspirational speaker, motivating professionals and business people in the pursuit of their life goals and missions. Feel free to contact Luis regarding how he can help you to further your mission.

Connect with Luis at:
www.AnswerIsLove.com
(702) 205-5385

Book Luis Rojas to Speak

If you are looking to have the people in your organization inspired to do more, be more, and love more, you need look no farther than Luis Rojas. He will not only leave your audience with a renewed passion for life, but they will come away with a deeper sense of what life is all about—loving one another.

Whether your audience is 10 or 10,000, in North America or abroad, Luis can deliver a customized message of inspiration for your small group, meeting, seminar, or international conference. Luis will share with you the deep truths he has learned from his life experiences, including his years as a prosecuting attorney and lawyer, and the wisdom he has acquired from the Universe.

Luis seeks to entertain audiences, make them laugh, perhaps make them cry, but most of all transform them into people who more deeply understand the human condition, the world, and their opportunity to spread love, joy, peace, and understanding to others. The result will be extraordinary change for individuals and your organization at large.

If you are looking for a memorable speaker who will leave your audience wanting more, contact Luis today at the information below. He will offer you a free thirty-minute consultation to determine how he can best serve your organization.

www.AnswerIsLove.com
SteinandRojas@yahoo.com
(702) 205-5385